Okpik: Cold-Weather Camping

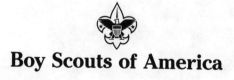

Boy Scouts of America

Contents

Okpik Leader Training
for Cold-Weather Camping

Cold-weather camping is any camping that takes place when the high temperature of the day is 50°F (10°C) or below. Conditions can include cold, wet, and windy weather. Hypothermia and dehydration can be serious problems. Other potential problems include frostnip or frostbite, immersion foot, and snow blindness.

Okpik: Cold Weather Camping can serve as the basis for a state-of-the-art training course designed to give the leader confidence in taking a small group into a cold environment, and support a year-round camping program. Cold-weather camping is appropriate only for those leaders and campers who already have basic Scouting skills and mild-weather camping experience.

This manual covers the skills and techniques that must be learned and the planning that must be done to ensure a successful, fun, and safe cold-weather camping experience. These include physical preparation, clothing, food and water, sanitation practices, first aid and emergency procedures, shelter and shelter building, methods of travel in snow, and making equipment. These must-know skills are important because cold-weather camping mistakes can be serious and certainly are not something upon which to build young Scouts' experience.

Leaders should use this manual with the video, *Winter Camping,* AV-010. The Venture handbook, *Snow Camping,* No. 3440, should be used as the Scout participant's manual.

The National Cold-Weather Camping Development Center of the Boy Scouts of America is located at the Northern Tier Base at Ely, Minn. This center provides materials and specializes in problems associated with cold-weather camping. The center shares this information with councils and other organizations through a variety of methods.

Health and safety procedures discussed in this manual have been reviewed by the Health and Safety Service at the BSA national office.

Chapter 1

The Fun of
Cold-Weather Camping

The Boy Scouts of America defines cold-weather camping as any camping that takes place when the high temperature of the day is 50°F (10°C) or below and is or could be involved with cold, wet, or windy conditions.

No camping is quite as challenging or exhilarating as that done in cold weather. Cold-weather camping is not just camping in the snow or camping in the mountains. It can be done anywhere that the temperature is 50°F (10°C) and below. It may involve hiking, backpacking, snowshoeing, or skiing; regardless, cold-weather camping is fun.

The Okpik Program

Okpik, the Boy Scouts of America's cold-weather camping program, was started at the Northern Tier National High Adventure Base at Ely, Minn. *Okpik* is the Inuit (North American Eskimo) name for the arctic or snowy owl. The arctic owl has been used as the symbol for the Okpik program since the early 1970s. Okpik is based on three traditional northern cultures, as well as the camping program of the Boy Scouts of America. The cultures of the Inuit, the North American Indian, and the Lapp, or Sami, of northern Europe have been used in developing the Okpik program. The program develops basic skills for cold-weather camping.

Inuit, the proper name for "North American Eskimo," is used throughout this handbook. The Inuit have given us many things for winter camping. Okpik clothing (especially the outerwear and footwear), snow goggles, snow scoop, and the cut-block igloo come from the Inuit, who live in the high Arctic of North America.

Snowshoes and the snow house, called a *quinzee,* are just two of the many items taken from the culture of the Indians who made their way from the warmer climates of North America to the snow toboggan climates of the far North.

Inuit (Eskimo) of North American Arctic

**North American Indian of the
Fur Trade Era**

Skis and the small sled called *ahkio* come from the people of Northern Europe, called Lapps or Laplanders. These people are reindeer herders and live in the northern part of Scandinavia and the Soviet Union. They are nomads who spend their lives following the reindeer. Since these people are always on the move, many of their travel techniques, as well as their clothing and equipment, are appropriate for cold-weather camping.

In 1927, the Boy Scouts of America published an experimental manual about winter camping. The introduction by James E. West and chapter 1 of that handbook are reproduced in Appendix A. The information is interesting and gives insight into the BSA camping style of many years ago. It is presented for its historical value, not as a training guide. Even though it is several decades old, there are parallels with the cold-weather camping methods of today.

Equivalent Temperatures

FAHRENHEIT	CELSIUS	FAHRENHEIT	CELSIUS
−40.0°F	−40.0°C	32.0°F	0.0°C
−30.0	−34.6	40.0	4.4
−20.0	−29.0	50.0	10.0
−10.0	−23.4	60.0	15.6
0.0	−17.8	70.0	21.1
10.0	−12.2	80.0	26.7
20.0	−6.8	90.0	32.2
30.0	−1.1	98.6	37.0

Fahrenheit to Celsius Conversion

Preparing for Cold-Weather Camping

The most important single point about cold-weather camping is that the cold is not as bad as it seems. Your attitude about the cold has a greater effect on your enjoyment of camping than does the weather. Thus, cold weather is no excuse for not camping. In fact, succeeding at cold-weather camping can be a source of great personal satisfaction. Cold can be unpleasant and may provide a good excuse for quitting, but a major hurdle is overcome once you learn to handle the cold and decide that it need not interfere with the fun of camping.

Danger of injury from the cold is minimal if campers follow the rules, use the skills outlined in this handbook, and use common sense. It is important for all campers to prepare before the trip, stick to assigned tasks, help others, and not let weather conditions interfere with the fun of camping.

Attention to the simple rules of good hygiene are necessary. You will be more comfortable if you keep clean and maintain good personal habits. These include washing your hands after using the toilet, brushing your teeth, and washing your body whenever possible.

A good, healthy appetite is another aid to staying comfortable. In the cold, your body burns up more food (calories) in order to keep you warm. It's a good idea to carry a snack for times when a little extra energy is needed.

Dry clothing is very important because once clothing becomes wet, it loses its insulation value. Planning ahead ensures that dry clothing is always available. Dry socks and underwear are especially important for your comfort.

Individuals, as well as the group, must be well organized for

The Laplander of Northern Europe

cold-weather camping. It is important to prepare good meals, proper shelters, and comfortable sleeping arrangements.

Remember that being organized at night will pay off in the morning. Because there is less light in the winter months, breakfast may have to be prepared in a low-light condition. In addition, snow is the north's greatest thief, because things left out of the shelter at night may not be visible the next morning if there has been even a light snow. Set aside tinder and kindling for fire-building where you can find it in the morning.

Protection from the temperature and from rain or snow is important in cold-weather camping. Wind protection must also be considered. Wind makes low temperatures feel even colder. The wind-chill chart on page 10 illustrates this problem. Knowing the effects of wind chill will help you plan your outings. Your plans should include plenty of warm clothing, adequate sleeping equipment, and good wind breaks, either natural or constructed.

Maintaining morale can be a problem during cold-weather camping. It takes extra effort to keep morale up and to relate to your group in the usual way. The following steps will help maintain morale:

- Be considerate of each other and try not to do anything unpleasant.

- Schedule plenty of fun time. Recreation is very important.

- Keep good track of your personal gear and keep it neat. Help keep shelters neat and clean. Dirty, untidy quarters lower morale.

- Make the camp one big group. Avoid the formation of groups or cliques. Everyone should take part in activities.

- Be sure that food for the trip is well-planned and adequate. Involve everyone in planning the menu. Make sure there are plenty of high-energy snacks.

- Plan a special or surprise event for the outing. Introduce a new game, a special snack, or something that will be fun for everyone.

Cold-Weather Activities

Planning is the key to having fun when camping in the cold. Camping in the cold can have all of the fun of warm-weather camping. Any campcraft can be done in the cold. Games may be even more enjoyable in cold weather. Star gazing takes on a new meaning in the cold, crisp air of winter. Storytelling is popular, as are campfires, in the evening. The question should not be, "What can we do?" but rather, "When can we go?"

WINDCHILL CHART

COOLING POWER OF WIND EXPRESSED AS "EQUIVALENT CHILL TEMPERATURE"

WIND SPEED		TEMPERATURE (°F)																				
KNOTS	MPH	40	35	30	25	20	15	10	5	0	-5	-10	-15	-20	-25	-30	-35	-40	-45	-50	-55	-60
		EQUIVALENT CHILL TEMPERATURE																				
CALM	CALM	40	35	30	25	20	15	10	5	0	-5	-10	-15	-20	-25	-30	-35	-40	-45	-50	-55	-60
3-6	5	35	30	25	20	15	10	5	0	-5	-10	-15	-20	-25	-30	-35	-40	-45	-50	-55	-60	-70
7-10	10	30	20	15	10	5	0	-10	-15	-20	-25	-35	-40	-45	-50	-60	-65	-70	-75	-80	-90	-95
11-15	15	25	15	10	0	-5	-10	-20	-25	-30	-40	-45	-50	-60	-65	-70	-80	-85	-90	-100	-105	-110
16-19	20	20	10	5	0	-10	-15	-25	-30	-35	-45	-50	-60	-65	-75	-80	-85	-95	-100	-110	-115	-120
20-23	25	15	10	0	-5	-15	-20	-30	-35	-45	-50	-60	-65	-75	-80	-90	-95	-105	-110	-120	-125	-135
24-28	30	10	5	0	-10	-20	-25	-30	-40	-50	-55	-65	-70	-80	-85	-95	-100	-110	-115	-125	-130	-140
29-32	35	10	5	-5	-10	-20	-30	-35	-40	-50	-60	-65	-75	-80	-90	-100	-105	-110	-120	-130	-135	-145
33-36	40	10	0	-5	-15	-20	-30	-35	-45	-55	-60	-70	-75	-85	-95	-100	-110	-115	-125	-130	-140	-150

WINDS ABOVE 40 MPH HAVE LITTLE ADDITIONAL EFFECT.

LITTLE DANGER

INCREASING DANGER
(Flesh may freeze within 1 minute.)

GREAT DANGER
(Flesh may freeze within 30 seconds.)

Chapter 2

Your Body and the Cold

Many sources of energy exist. The sun is one, but it doesn't always shine. The wind is another, but often there is no breeze. Electricity is a third, but it's not always available. There is, however, one source of energy that is always plentiful. It is inexpensive and easy to use, yet it is overlooked by most campers. What is this source of energy? Body heat. Your body is its own heating plant. Food, water, and oxygen are its fuels.

The body is a complex machine that depends upon chemical and muscular activity to sustain life. It works best when it is regularly fed, rested, and kept at a steady temperature of 98.6°F (37°C).

Understanding how your body reacts to slight internal temperature differences enables you to respond more quickly to changes in your comfort. Your body is always giving signals that tell you if you are too warm or too cold. If you are attuned to these, you can respond appropriately and remain comfortable for long periods of time, even in extreme conditions.

Homeostasis

Homeostasis is the medical term for the process controlling the equilibrium of your body's temperature. To function properly, your body must maintain an even temperature (98.6°F or 37°C) around the vital organs within your torso. A few degrees too high or too low can allow serious illness and, if unchecked, death.

The homeostatic process functions as your body's thermostat, using your arms and legs to radiate heat away from your torso, like the cooling vents on a car's radiator. When your body is producing more than enough heat to maintain a core temperature of 98.6°F (37°C) around the vital organs in the torso, the homeostatic process dilates the blood vessels in your arms, legs, hands, and feet to allow full blood flow to the skin surfaces of your extremities.

When cold threatens your body temperature equilibrium, the homeostatic process constricts these blood vessels, decreasing blood flow to your extremities. Blood flow to the fingers and toes can be cut back as much as 99 percent or more. This is why your hands and feet get numb when you're cold, and why they're particularly vulnerable to frostbite.

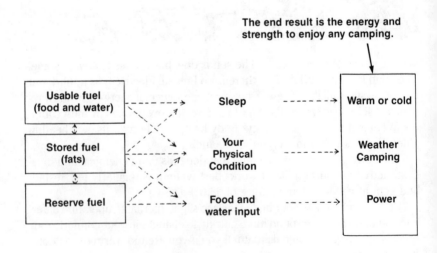

Generation of Heat and Comfort

Since your brain needs oxygen to function, your body can't cut off the flow of blood to your head in order to conserve heat. Consequently, much of your body heat can be lost through an uncovered head and neck. Wearing a hat can also keep your hands and feet warm. Because your hat reduces the loss of body heat through your head, your body can afford to send more body heat to your extremities. Minimizing body-heat loss is vital in cold-weather camping because continued loss of body heat at a rate faster than your body can produce it results in hypothermia.

How Your Body Loses Heat

Radiation. Radiation is a leading cause of heat loss in almost any situation. The head is the most efficient part of the body's radiator system. So rapid is the radiation from the head in a cold situation that heat loss from an unprotected, uncovered head can be enormous. An unprotected head may lose up to one-half of the body's total heat production at 40°F (4°C), and up to three-quarters of total body heat production at 5°F (−15°C). Remember the maxim, "When your feet are cold, put on your hat." Parkas with attached hoods or balaclavas are essential for protection against this dramatic heat loss in cold, windy, or wet situations.

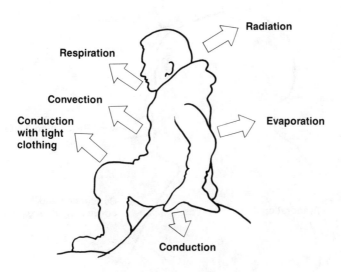

Types of Body Heat Loss

Conduction. Ordinarily, only small amounts of body heat are lost by conduction. But winter campers tend to lose body heat this way more than others do because they often carry metal tools such as a saw, axe, or shovel, and they often rest by sitting on ice, snow, or cold rock. Climbing ungloved over cold rock is another mechanism of heat loss through conduction.

Conduction of heat from skin to metal is so rapid it can produce an actual cementing of skin to metal, instantly freezing the skin's surface moisture to the metal, with subsequent frostbite or loss of skin. Wearing thin silk or cotton gloves when handling metal (axe, saw, camera, stove, shovel) protects against this freezing hazard.

Handling gasoline or other liquid fuels at low temperatures is especially dangerous. Gasoline stored in a metal canister outside of the tent during a storm will cool to the lowest temperature attained during the storm. Even covered with an insulating blanket of snow, it cannot rewarm, so when it is uncovered, its temperature may be as low as −20° to −40°F (−29° to −40°C). Spilling such supercooled fluids on your hands will cause instant frostbite. This happens not only from the conduction of heat by cold liquid, but also by the further cooling effect of rapid evaporation of the liquid as it hits the skin. Many cases of severe frostbite occur in this manner.

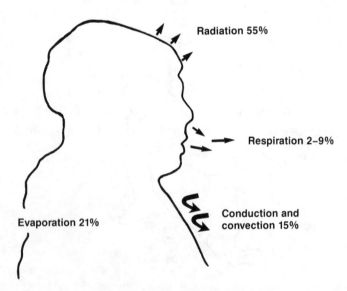

Types and Possible Percentages of Upper-Body Heat Loss

Convection. Convection is an active avenue of body heat escape in the outdoors. By radiation, the body continuously warms a thin layer of air next to the skin to a temperature nearly equal to that of the skin. If this warm-air layer is retained close to the body by clothing, you remain warm. However, if this warm layer of air is constantly being removed by a brisk wind (convection), you feel cool and have to put on more clothing.

In short, the primary function of clothing is to retain a layer of warm air close to your body. In conditions of severe cold and wind, you need garments of high wind resistance and insulating qualities.

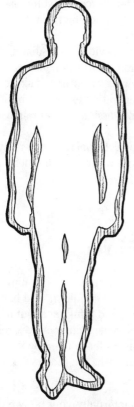

This drawing shows the layer of warm air next to the body. When disturbed by wind or other influences, the loss of this layer causes the body to cool.

Evaporation. The evaporation of sweat from the skin and the insensible evaporation of water from the skin and lungs account for a substantial loss of body heat. There is very little you can do to prevent this loss. In fact, those in the outdoors are well advised to help the process of evaporation by wearing fabrics that "breathe." If water vapor cannot pass freely through your clothing, it condenses and freezes.

The famous Arctic explorer, Fridtjof Nansen, made this observation in 1898: "During the course of the day the damp exhalations of the body had little by little condensed in our outer garments, which were now a mass of ice and transformed into complete suits of ice armor." Nansen and his men were wearing nonporous outer garments of animal skins.

Respiration. Inhaling cool air and exhaling warm air accounts for a significant amount of heat loss. This is especially true at high altitudes, at low temperatures, and during heavy exertion. There is little you can do to prevent or conserve this type of heat loss. Your breath helps to warm a tent or snow cave, if you have one, but that's about the extent of its thermal value.

How Weather Affects Heat Loss

Wind Chill. If there were no breeze at all (a rare occurrence on mountains), you could remain lightly clad and comfortable at 0°F for long periods of time. But let the air stir even slightly, and the calories or heat energy produced by your body will go, go, go.

Water Chill. The thermal conductivity of water (or ice) is 20 times as great as that of still air. This means that wet clothing can extract heat from your body much faster than clean, dry clothing.

When your clothing gets wet, it no longer provides an insulating layer of warm air next to the skin. Instead, it rapidly conducts heat away from your body and dissipates it into the environment. Wet clothing is like a wick. If a cold wind is blowing, or if you are not generating extra heat by strong exertion, this "wicking action" or "water chill" dissipates heat much more rapidly than your body can produce it.

It is worth noting that the wicking action of wet wool is considerably less than that of other fabrics. Wool provides some warmth even when damp.

The Secrets of Keeping Warm

People acclimated to winter conditions know the importance of eating properly, getting adequate rest, being in good physical condition, and having a positive mental attitude. The more time you spend thinking about miserable conditions, the harder adaptation becomes. When winter arrives, remind yourself that little can be done about it. Instead, learn to enjoy it.

The people who really enjoy the colder months are those who do the following:

- Keep the body core warm. When you cool internally, your body reduces the amount of blood circulating to the extremities. It is important to keep activity rate and clothing appropriate for the weather conditions. This assures adequate warmth throughout your body.

- Make sure blood circulates freely. Most of your heat is generated in your head, trunk, and muscles. The blood then warms your entire body by flowing unrestricted to the extremities. That's why it is important to avoid snug or tight-fitting garments, especially hand- and footwear.

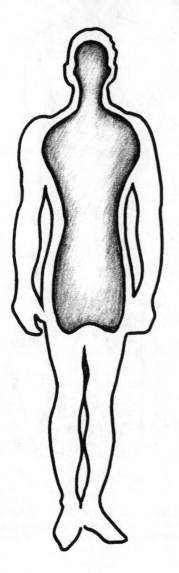

- Select the proper type and amount of clothing. Regulate your clothing according to your activity rate. This is the most effective way to ensure comfort.
- Pay attention to internal signals. Don't wait until you are cold to put on more clothing. Act when you first begin to feel cooler.

Your body can get used to almost any condition over a period of time, usually in a couple of weeks. Exposure to cold weather should be slow at first, then gradually increased. Soon you will feel at home even in the coldest weather.

We've already discussed how the body generates heat and how it loses it. Developing an understanding of insulation in clothing will help you learn to retain your body heat more efficiently.

Body Core—The core of the body includes all internal organs. This is the heat producing mechanism that must stay at 98.6°F (37°C) to keep the rest of the body warm.

Types and Amounts of Clothing

1. long underwear; 2. shirt or inner layer; 3. sweater or light jacket; 4. wind or rain gear; 5. inner pants; 6. wind or rain pants; 7. wicker inner socks; 8. insulating socks; 9. boot liners; 10. and 11. footwear; 12. and 13. head coverings; 14. and 15. gloves and mittens

Using Insulation

Insulation is any material that traps air and doesn't allow it to move around freely. This trapped air is called "dead air." A good example of an insulator is a vacuum bottle. It insulates by trapping layers of air between the outside wall and the inner vessel (which holds the food or beverage), and can keep cold foods cold and hot foods hot. It is important to understand that insulation doesn't differentiate between cold and hot; it retains either temperature. And insulation doesn't generate any heat. You must be active enough to generate the heat necessary for your garments to keep you warm. As a result, the more active you are, the less insulation you require. A T-shirt might be adequate for strenuous outside work in the fall, while a shirt and sweater are required for a less energetic indoor activity such as reading.

The term *insulation,* as we use it in cold-weather camping, means the ability to hold dead air. This ability is affected by several factors. Moisture is the greatest concern, since we lose heat to moisture much faster than to dry air. Since many items of clothing hold moisture, the following information may prove helpful.

Natural fibers (cotton, wool, linen, and silk) are proteins. They are also *hydrophiles;* they absorb water in the cell structure of their fibers. Cotton absorbs a great deal more than wool. This lesser degree of absorption in wool prompts the saying "wool is warm, even when wet." Nothing is warm, however, when frozen!

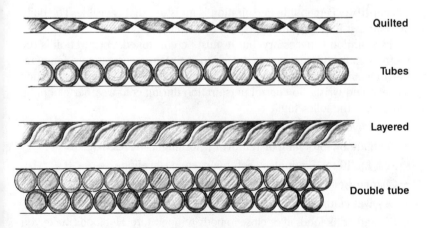

Quilted

Tubes

Layered

Double tube

Types of Garment and Sleeping Bag Insulation

Most synthetics used as winter-clothing insulation are not hydrophilic, but instead are hydrophobic. *Hydrophobic* means that these fibers have no ability to combine with or dissolve in water. Polypropylene, an excellent moisture "wicker" used primarily in underwear, absorbs less than one percent of its weight in moisture, as do many piles, dacrons, etc. This is about one-sixth the absorption of wool. These synthetics are generally much easier to dry since they hold water only on the surface of the fiber, not in the cell structure. (The holding of moisture or dead air on the fiber is called *capillarity.)*

Controlling Perspiration

Perspiration is the greatest cause of moisture buildup in clothing. Outside moisture such as rain, sleet, or snow can be taken care of with proper clothing.

Your body is cooled by three types of perspiration—insensible, nonperceptible, and perceptible. The hypothalamus, the lower portion of the brain, controls all three types of perspiration.

Insensible. Your body loses from one to one-and-a-half pints of fluid each day in the form of insensible perspiration. This perspiration is generally not visible and exists basically to maintain skin flexibility.

Nonperceptible. This invisible moisture evaporates and cools as it leaves the skin surface. The daily amount lost is variable.

Perceptible. Perceptible perspiration is moisture that is visible. The daily amount lost in perceptible perspiration is variable.

Perspiration is necessary, but it must be controlled. Perspiration is the method your body uses to cool itself to maintain a correct core temperature of 98.6°F (37°C). It is controlled by ventilation of body thermostats such as head and wrists. To control perspiration during cold-weather camping, remember the following:

• Don't over-exercise—take it easy.

• Ventilate by loosening or removing clothing as necessary.

• Rest for 10 to 15 minutes each hour when traveling.

• Change wet layers of clothing before they soak other layers.

• Dry wet clothing.

• Eat and drink foods at or close to body temperature. Hot foods make you perspire; cold foods rob your body of heat.

The Key to Keeping Warm is the Word COLD

Keep C-O-L-D to stay warm. COLD may not seem like the key to keeping warm, but it is if you look at it this way:

keep **C**lean

avoid **O**verheating

wear **L**ayers

stay **D**ry

Remember this key; it will help you learn techniques for staying warm while camping in cold weather.

Chapter 3

Clothing and Sleeping Systems

Clothing and bedding needs for cold-weather camping must be considered carefully. Decisions should be based on the conditions expected during the campout. Selections should also be flexible enough to adjust to varying conditions.

Types of Cold

There are basically three types of cold: wet, dry, and Arctic-like. Wet cold is the most dangerous, and it is the type of cold in which most winter camping is done. Wet-cold temperatures range from 50°F (10°C) to 14°F (−10°C). Wet cold can occur either with or without snow. Dry-cold temperatures vary from 14°F (−10°C) to −20°F (−29°C). Dry cold is usually associated with snow conditions. In Arctic-like cold, temperatures are below −20°F (−29°C). Rarely, if ever, would you encounter temperatures this low without snow. Each type of cold requires different clothing considerations.

Wet Cold. During wet-cold conditions, temperature differences between the warmest time of the day and the coldest period at night may be as great as 30° or 40°F. The coldest temperature usually occurs about 1 hour before dawn, unless there is a strong frontal system affecting the weather. This wide temperature fluctuation causes melting during the day and a hard freeze at night. The cycle of freezing and thawing, often accompanied by rain or wet snow, causes the ground to become muddy or even slushy. Wet-cold clothing is designed to cope with these conditions.

Dry Cold. During dry-cold conditions, the ground is usually frozen and the snow cover is relatively dry, in the form of small crystals. Strong winds cause the low temperatures to seem colder and increase the need for protecting the entire body. Dry-cold clothing is the same as for wet-cold conditions except that more insulating layers are added, and the rain protection needed in wet-cold conditions can be replaced by windproof outer clothing that is water repellent.

Arctic-like Cold. Arctic-like cold requires the most insulation, especially when you are not active. During times of Arctic-like cold, many thermally formed materials (metals, plastics, etc.) change their physical properties, becoming brittle; they may break or shatter. Camping comfortably at these temperatures takes a great deal of experience. The correct layering of clothing is essential. The outer layer should be a windproof barrier that covers most of the body.

The Okpik Clothing System

The Inuit refer to all warm clothing as *okkortok*. The Okpik system is similar to the many-layered clothing the Inuit call the *annorak*.

- The outer coat is called *kolliktark*.
- The inner coat is called *attagi*.
- Trousers are called *karklik*.
- All undergarments or liners are *illupak*.
- Boots are *kamiks,* socks are *alerte,* and mittens are *poaluk*.

The Inuit

You need clothing that protects you from the cold and holds your body heat, but that also can be ventilated. The layers should be thin so frost forms between layers, not inside the insulation.

Clothes for cold-weather camping should be designed so that the camper can function effectively in any environment. The prime consideration is comfort, not appearance. The clothing is designed to keep campers warm rather than stylish. However, the three principles of insulation, layering, and ventilation used in the Okpik system apply to any cold-weather clothing.

Okpik clothing design incorporates the principles of insulation, layering, and ventilation to make the clothing work for the wearer. Insulation material reduces the amount of body heat lost to the outside. By regulating the amount of insulation, you regulate the amount of heat lost or retained. This flexibility becomes important when environmental conditions or activities change, altering the amount of warmth needed for comfort and safety.

One method of insulation is layering. Several layers of medium-weight clothing provide more insulation and flexibility than one heavy garment. This is true even if the heavy garment is as thick as the combined layers. This is possible because air is trapped between each clothing layer, as well as in the air pockets between the cloth fibers, as it is warmed by body heat. To capitalize on this, the layers of clothing are designed differently. Winter underwear is porous, with many air pockets to hold body-warmed air, while the outer garments are made of windproof, water-repellent fabric to keep cold air outside. The layering method allows greater freedom of movement and is easily adjusted for a wide range of conditions. Layers can simply be added or subtracted as needed.

Ventilation helps to maintain a comfortable body temperature. It is important to ventilate before you become overheated, because evaporating perspiration cools the body. Perspiration can also fill the air spaces of your clothing with moisture-laden air, reducing its insulating qualities. Scientists

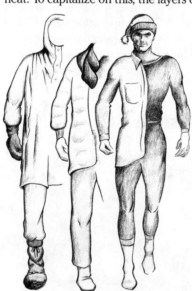

A Proper System of Layering

advise, "Allow outside air to cool overheated layers by adjusting openings such as cuffs and front closures. If more cooling is necessary, it may be time to remove a layer."

The illustrations on the following pages show an outer clothing system based on layering that works well in most cold-weather camping, whether in wet-cold, dry-cold, or Arctic-like conditions. Layers are important, as they supply the insulation necessary to control the body's warmth. They can also be adequately ventilated to control the buildup of perspiration within the clothing. This clothing system uses layers that fit over one another loosely and without constricting body movement. The outer garments should be water-repellent or, in areas of extreme wetness during wet-cold conditions, both breathable and waterproof.

The wind parka pullover (not insulated), insulated parka liner, insulated vest with removable sleeves, hood, trousers, insulated trouser liner, wind pant, and insulated wind pant liner make up the Okpik outer clothing system. They are used with various inner layers and footwear, including the mukluk with foam or conventional liners, and upper-body protection. This upper-body protection includes cheek protectors, hat or cap, balaclava, scarf, headover, hand protection with gloves, wristlets, mittens, and protective overmittens. Sleeping attire is discussed under Cold-Weather Sleeping Systems.

Hood

Wind parka pullover

Removable sleeve

Vest

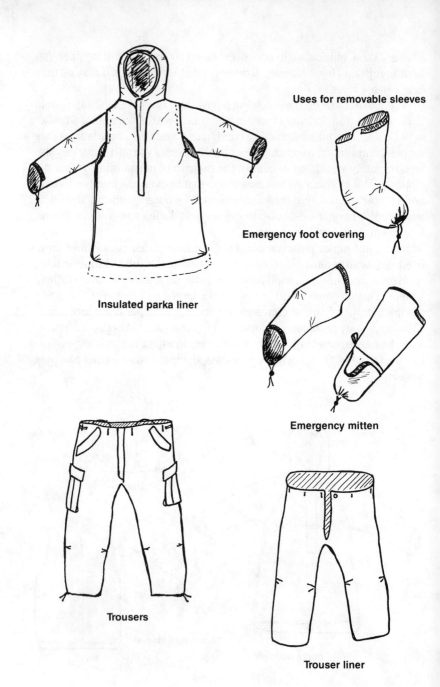

Insulated parka liner

Uses for removable sleeves

Emergency foot covering

Emergency mitten

Trousers

Trouser liner

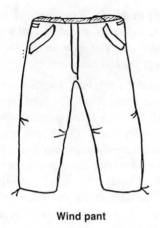

Wind pant

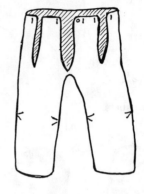

Wind pant liner

Inner Layers and Footwear

Socks. Wear a wicking (polypropylene or similar material) sock next to your foot. The insulating socks can be made of wool or wool blends. You may want to consider a vapor barrier sock as well. If you use a vapor barrier sock, place it between the wicking socks and the insulating socks.

Long Underwear. Use long underwear made from a wicking-type material such as polypropylene.

Pants. Good wool pants are hard to beat as cold-weather clothing items. Figure-eight suspenders work well and allow you to change or add wind pants without taking off the upper garments.

"A"-style suspenders

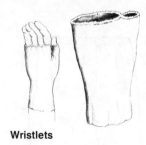

Wristlets

Scarf

Cheek protector

Upper-Body Protection. Use layers of shirts, sweaters, and vests. Make sure you wear items that fit properly and are comfortable.

Hand Protection. Nothing can be more frustrating than cold hands. Use wristlets to keep your whole hand, especially your fingers, warm. Mittens are warmer than gloves, but you may prefer gloves if you are skiing or using your hands for other work. Both inner and outer mitts may be necessary, so don't forget extras.

Neck Protection. Be sure that you have either a scarf or neck gaiter to protect your throat and neck area. The 5- or 6-foot tubular scarf can be used in several different ways, including as an emergency cap or sleeping hood.

Cheek Protection. See the chapter on making equipment for instructions on making cheek protectors.

Headgear. Caps, ear warmers, hats, etc., are important because they minimize the heat loss from your head.

Footwear. Among the most important items in footwear are insulated insoles. These can be made from scraps of foam or they can be purchased in sporting goods stores.

Make sure your footwear meets the requirements of the area where you camp. Always carry extra footwear to use in camp. Don't make the mistake of wearing boots that are too tight. For snow camping, consider mukluks or other snow boots. Make sure you wear them properly. Snow boots must be worn with insoles as well as socks or footwraps. Make sure you have plenty of insulation and that your footwear allows adequate circulation.

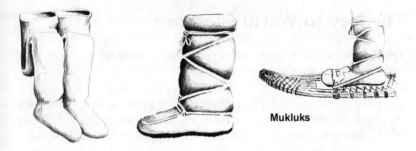

Mukluks

Proper method of using an insole or insoles with a foot wrap inside a mukluk

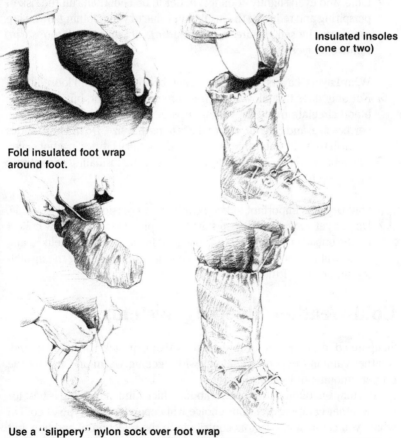

Insulated insoles (one or two)

Fold insulated foot wrap around foot.

Use a "slippery" nylon sock over foot wrap and insert in mukluk or other cold-weather foot gear.

Mukluk

The Key to Warm Clothing

The **C-O-L-D** key to keeping warm applies to the clothing you wear. Here are some of the ways you can use it:

C — Keep **C**lothing Clean. Dirt and grease clog the air spaces in the clothing and reduce its insulation value. When cleaning, make sure all soap is rinsed out because soap residue can reduce insulation qualities.

O — Avoid **O**verheating. Select the clothes that you need to stay comfortable, and even slightly cool. It is better to be cool than run the risk of perspiring and reducing the insulation value of your clothing. If you are too warm, loosen closures a few at a time; if you are still too warm, remove a layer.

L — Wear **L**ayers. Layers of clothing should be worn long and loose-fitting. Not only does this allow more freedom of movement, but it lets your blood circulate freely, preventing frostbite. Select clothing that is the correct size, and care for it so that it retains that size. Do not boil fabrics or wash them in water that is too hot. Do not dry fabrics in a hot dryer. The fabrics will shrink and clothes will lose the insulating advantages of a loose fit.

D — Stay **D**ry. It is important to keep clothing dry outside as well as inside. Do not get so warm that you start to perspire. Do not let snow collect on the outside of your clothing. The heat from your body melts it, and some will penetrate even water-repellent fabric, reducing the insulating properties of the fabric.

Cold-Weather Sleeping Systems

Sleeping condition is one of three factors that can make or break a cold-weather camping experience, along with keeping warm and having the proper amounts of food and water.

You may encounter controversy about which kind of bedding is best for cold-weather camping, but your choice will depend on the type of cold in which you camp. Many factors contribute to the selection of bedding, but the following points apply to all cold-weather camping situations:

- The body cools down during sleep. The blood (heat) is drawn from the extremities (feet and hands) and brought to the center, or core, of the body.

- In all cold-weather camping situations, the ground is colder than the body. Proper insulation must be provided to prevent heat loss by conduction.

- **C-O-L-D,** the key to staying warm, is as important with bedding as it is with clothing.

C Your bedding should have a washable liner so that it stays **C**lean.

O To keep you from **O**verheating, your bedding must be ventilated. Overheating in a sleeping bag produces perspiration just as when you wear the wrong clothing.

L Your bedding should be lightweight and large enough to accommodate you. If possible, use a **L**ayered system. When a layered system is used, it is easier to remove the frost buildup that occurs naturally when your body produces warmth. It is a major concern if you are camping for more than one night.

D Keep your equipment as **D**ry as possible by pumping all of the warm, moist air out of the bag each morning and then airing and exposing it to the radiant warmth of the sun. Turn the bag or bags inside-out and check for frost. Then leave them open until they cool to the air temperature.

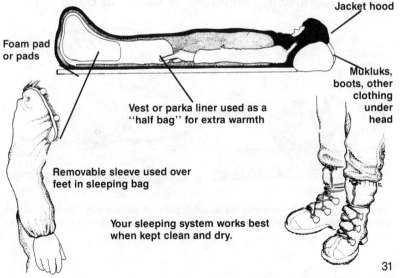

Jacket hood

Foam pad
or pads

Mukluks,
boots, other
clothing
under
head

Vest or parka liner used as a
"half bag" for extra warmth

Removable sleeve used over
feet in sleeping bag

Your sleeping system works best
when kept clean and dry.

Selecting the proper cold-weather bedding is not simple—there are many sleeping bags on the market. Learn all you can about your camping climate and conditions, and use this chapter to help you choose the combination of pieces that will be the most comfortable sleeping system for you.

When preparing sleeping equipment for cold weather campouts, consider the temperature and the type of cold you expect to encounter. Most cold-weather camping is done in wet-cold or dry-cold conditions, not in Arctic-like cold, and the temperature in a shelter is rarely below zero. In those conditions, a layered sleeping system protects you against cold and makes it easier to control moisture and heat.

A cold-weather sleeping system includes some or all of these elements, depending on the particular situation: insulation between the outer sleeping bag and the ground or floor; a sleeping bag or layers of bags; a washable sleeping bag liner; a sleeping suit; loose socks or other foot insulators; a stocking cap; wristlets; and a tubular scarf.

Ground or Floor Insulation. The insulation under the sleepers is the most critical concern. Good insulation should cover the entire floor of the sleeping quarters rather than just a small area under each sleeper. With the floor of the shelter completely covered, you do not have to worry about sleepers

Controlling Moisture in Sleeping Bags

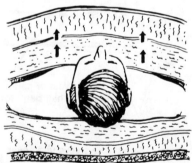

Frost forms when moisture hits the freezing point. A double bag passes moisture more efficiently. Frost will usually form between layers—not inside insulation as with the single bag.

rolling off the pads. Using this method, you minimize the entire shelter's heat loss not only by conduction, but also by radiation and convection.

The conductive heat loss from your body to the colder ground is subtle and usually not easily recognized. This heat loss drains the body of warmth and eventually makes sleeping impossible. A problem with recognizing heat loss to the ground is that you usually feel warm next to the colder surface, even as you lose heat to it.

Adequate protection under a sleeping bag requires a minimum of ⅜- to ½-inch thickness of a good, firm insulation. A 1-inch thick open-cell foam pad is not adequate; it gives much less than half of this at the pressure points (hips, shoulders, feet, etc.). The open-cell foam sleeping pad is designed to provide comfort, not insulation. It can be used on top of another pad, but is inadequate by itself.

Sleeping Bags. In choosing a sleeping bag, make sure of your needs and wants, considering the temperature where you will camp. Ask others to give you honest answers as to how their bags work in your camping locality. Synthetic insulation can be very good in sleeping bags; synthetics pick up little moisture, and can be washed easily. If you use a down bag in combination with other sleeping bags, always make sure it is the bag closest to the body. The warm air leaving your body is moist. As it cools, it loses its ability to hold moisture, and the moisture condenses. Since down is porous, it absorbs this moisture; synthetics, being less porous, let the moisture pass more readily.

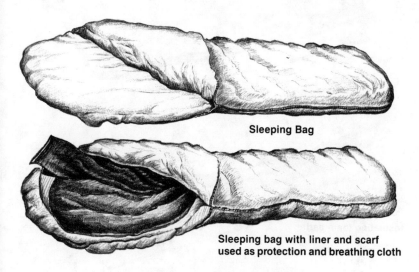

Sleeping Bag

Sleeping bag with liner and scarf used as protection and breathing cloth

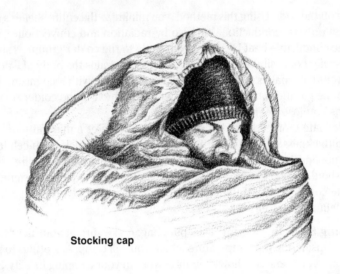

Stocking cap

Double bag with removable liner

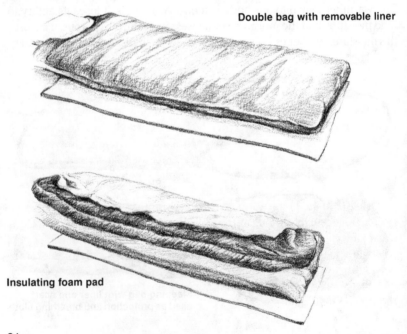

Insulating foam pad

The elephant foot or half-bag helps to conserve your body heat while you sleep. It is form-fitting but not tight, and goes over inner items, closing with a drawstring under the arms. This bag can be made of many different materials. The half-bag moves with you and helps keep a warm envelope of air around your lower body.

Washable, Insulating Liner. This completes your sleeping bag combination. The Boy Scouts of America Supply Division has several good selections. If the liner is only for use during cold-weather camping, try the no-zipper model. This style helps even more to enclose that warm envelope of air around you. (Zippers and other openings are just another place for heat loss.) This liner, as well as the other sleeping items, should be washed often. Keeping your sleeping equipment clean and dry goes a long way toward keeping you warm.

Sleeping Attire. Keeping your feet warm is usually the biggest problem when sleeping in cold weather. Before retiring, be sure your feet are as dry as possible. This can be done by "dry" washing with a good foot powder. The best foot powder contains a high percentage of aluminum chlorohydrate. This substance dries the skin and shrinks the pores to reduce normal perspiration. Wear a loose insulator on your feet for sleeping. Socks can be used, but be sure they are dry and are not tight. The constriction of a tight pair of socks is enough to cut off the warmth generated by the blood flowing to the feet.

Other sleeping attire is dictated by the degree of cold encountered on your outing. Use a "sleeping suit," either a clean, dry set of long underwear or pajamas, when cold-weather camping. The new long underwear made from a family of polymers that include polypropylene works quite well. A major attribute of these products is their ability to continue to wick moisture away from the body even at the skin temperature of a sleeping person. Since the conductive heat loss of water is high in cold-weather camping conditions, this is of major importance.

Other clothing items normally worn for protection during the day can also be used at night, as long as they are clean and dry. Some of these include a stocking cap, which prevents heat loss that continues even during sleep; wristlets, which are very helpful in keeping hands warm; and a tubular scarf, which can be used for protection in several ways. A tubular scarf is an excellent choice since it can be made into a cap, pulled on the feet, arms, or even the legs if necessary.

Chapter 4

Food, Water, and Sanitation

Food, water, and sanitation are important considerations for cold-weather camping. Food should be easy to prepare and provide the calories and bulk necessary to provide you with heat and energy, as well as supply needed nutrients. Plans should be made to collect and purify water as needed. Finally, eating and drinking necessitate plans for sanitary waste elimination.

Nutrition

Except under survival conditions, well-clothed, sheltered, and trained campers use little more food in the cold than in moderate temperatures. However, caloric intake in cold weather increases for two reasons. First, the extra activity required by dressing and the hampering effect and weight of that clothing increases energy needs. Second, the stimulus of the cold gives you a ravenous appetite. However, because the body "fires" burn somewhat hotter in cold weather and because food affects morale, you will want to supply your group well.

Foods come from animal and vegetable sources, and serve three functions in the body:

• Serve as fuel to provide heat energy or calories.

• Provide materials for building, repairing, or maintaining body tissues.

• Help regulate body processes.

Calories measure the amount of energy in the food you eat. They are furnished by carbohydrates, fats, and proteins.

Carbohydrates. Carbohydrates are the main source of energy. They are grouped together as starches, sugars, and celluloses. Starches and sugars are quick-energy foods because they provide only energy. Starches are found in bread, cereals, flour, and potatoes. Sources of sugar in the diet include ordinary white or brown sugar, milk, and fruit. During digestion, starches and sugars are turned into simple sugars which are then oxidized to give energy. The body does not digest cellulose (dietary fiber), but fiber helps move food wastes through the digestive tract, making them easier to pass. The best sources of fiber are whole grain cereals and breads, nuts, seeds, fruits, and vegetables.

Fats. Fats are the highest energy food, providing about 9 calories per gram. Carbohydrates and proteins each provide about 4 calories per gram in metabolism. They also furnish the natural sources for the fat-soluble vitamins A, D, E, and K. Fats can be either animal or vegetable in origin. Fats give a diet its "staying" qualities, helping to satisfy your appetite.

Fats and carbohydrates are called "protein sparers" since their presence prevents the body from having to burn its protein (blood and muscle) to give energy. The body selects carbohydrates to burn first, then fat, then protein, because of their relative ease of metabolism. A diet consisting of 40 percent fat, 40 percent carbohydrates, and 20 percent protein appears to be best in cold weather, for a number reasons.

Protein. Protein is the most common substance, other than water, in your body. Its main function is the growth and maintenance of body structures. Supplying energy is a backup function for protein. Carbohydrates and fats have the primary responsibility for supplying energy. Protein serves this function only if not enough of those nutrients are available to meet the body's energy needs. Protein can be either of animal or vegetable origin. Proteins are made of building blocks called amino acids. Most of the amino acids can be manufactured in your body, but some cannot, so these essential amino acids must be supplied by the foods you eat. Protein from animal sources (meat, fish, poultry, milk, and eggs) supply all of the essential amino acids. Protein from vegetable sources (beans, peas, whole grains, and nuts) may have several of the essential amino acids, but rarely all of them.

Protein has another remarkable property: the specific dynamic action by which protein, in its own digestion and oxidation, increases body metabolism by 30 percent. This is a source of heat in addition to that normally produced by the muscles and the liver. In the cold, protein is an additionally protective food. Because the byproducts of protein metabolism are dependent on the kidney for excretion, water intake must be kept up to prevent damaging hard-worked kidneys when increased protein is eaten. This liquid can be in almost any form (water, fruit drinks, hot thin soups), except coffee. Not only does coffee increase nervous tension in cold climates, but it also causes excess dehydration by stimulating kidney function. This decreases the body's ability to handle protein excretion.

Provisioning

Using *Best and Taylor's Physiological Basis of Medical Practice* as a reference, the best average temperate-climate diet follows, along with a recommended cold-weather diet.

Food Element	Temperate Climate	Cold Weather
Carbohydrates (4.1 calories/gram)	53%	40%
Fats (9.2 calories/gram)	35%	40%
Proteins (4.1 calories/gram) (first-class proteins: meat, milk, eggs)	12%	20%

The number of calories required per day is based on many factors and should be matched to the individual and the circumstances.

The quantity of calories utilized in winter programs depends on many factors: weather, temperature, type of activity, etc. The following example of a day's ration is designed to be adjusted from between 3,000 and 4,000-plus calories per day.

This ration should be consumed along with $2^1/_2$ to 3 quarts of water per day. The amount of water can be increased depending upon the amount of work, the temperature, etc.

Breakfast

Breakfast should provide a moderate amount of energy but enough fat to satisfy your appetite. A good breakfast might include:

- Hot cereals—oat, wheat, rice, corn, grits, etc.
- Cake bar or granola bars.
- Fruit—a single item like raisins or mixed fruit. Sauce can be added to make a fruit soup.
- Fruit juice—a pure fruit juice, not a fruit-flavored drink as is used for lunch and dinner. The primary purpose of this juice is to provide liquid, sugar for energy, and vitamin C.
- Hot drink—can be cocoa, but should not be limited to this product alone. Other good hot breakfast drinks include tea, eggnog, and spiced hot cider.

Breakfast Preparation. Hot cereals can be either cooked or instant. A variety of preparation methods can be used, including use of a fireless cooker for overnight cooking. Cereals should be sweetened with honey or brown sugar, with refined white sugar being a last choice. Wheat germ can be added to any cereal to increase its nutrient value. The fat for breakfast comes mainly from butter or margarine added to hot cereal. Corn oil margarine is a good choice.

Dry fruit can be eaten as is or made into fruit soup by adding a sauce and hot water. Cake bars are high in carbohydrates and supply needed energy in the morning. They can also be broken up and added to cereal.

Fruit juice can be consumed either hot or cold. If it is to be served hot, add the mix to hot, but not boiling, water. Boiling destroys vitamin C. Prepare the hot drink according to instructions, remembering that the hotter the drink is, the more likely your body will sweat to cool itself. A warm drink is better than an extremely hot drink.

Lunch

Lunch should provide high-carbohydrate energy with a minimum of preparation. A good lunch will include:

- Hard, fortified crackers or Hudson Bay Bread.
- Spread for crackers—peanut butter, honey, jelly, etc.
- Fruit drink, hot or cold
- Hot soup or other hot dish—baked beans, etc.
- Fruit—applesauce, etc.
- Trail snack

Lunch Preparation. Lunch items should be prepared ahead, or require little or no preparation, so they can be eaten during the morning and early afternoon as well as at a specific time. At a midday halt, a hot drink or soup can be prepared. Retort baked beans and applesauce are excellent lunch items. Place individually packaged spreads between clothing layers to thaw before pausing for lunch.

Hudson Bay Bread

Hudson Bay Bread is a year-round favorite, serving as the basis of a high-energy lunch or snack. Start by mixing together the following ingredients:

1½ lbs. margarine or butter	2 tsp. maple flavoring
4 cups sugar	Then mix in:
⅔ cup corn syrup	1½ cups ground nuts
⅔ cup honey	19 cups oatmeal

Spread the mixture in a large sheet pan. Press it down into the pan. Bake at 325°F in a wind oven for 15 to 18 minutes. As soon as the bread is taken from the oven, use a spatula to press it down (to keep it from crumbling). Cut the bread while it is still warm.

For home preparation, cut the recipe at least in half. A conventional oven requires a longer baking time.

Dinner

Dinner should provide adequate calories and the highest amount of protein of the day. This provides warmth and promotes tissue repair during the night's rest. A dinner menu should include the following:

- Hot main dish—can be a one-dish meal, a retort meal, or a freeze-dried dinner, and should include a starch (rice, noodles, or potatoes), a sauce (meat broth, gravies, etc.), and a meat (chicken, beef, or ham).
- Freeze-dried or fresh vegetables are served separately or added to the main dish.
- Crackers—can be less "durable" than those eaten at lunch, but should still be high in nutritional value.
- Fruit drink—same as lunch item; 8-ounce serving.
- Hot drink—same as at breakfast; a 1-cup serving.
- Dessert—can be one that requires preparation and cooling, such as a pudding, or an already prepared item. A hot sauce goes well with either.
- Extras—Sugar or sweetener, milk powder, cream powder, salt, pepper, and your own favorite spices. Butter or margarine, honey, maple sugar, fruit soup mixes, flavored teas, instant hot soups and bouillons, special soups, extra snack items such as fruits and nuts. Adults may want coffee and tea. Don't forget paper towels and matches!

Dinner Preparation. Dinner is, by far, the most complicated meal of your winter camping day. At-home preparation makes it easier. If you plan to make a meal on the trail from scratch, make certain you have at least practiced it at home on the stove.

Most one-pot dishes begin by boiling lightly salted water. If you use fresh meats or vegetables, cook them in the boiling water before adding the starch. Otherwise, add the starch (rice, noodles, or potatoes) to the boiling water and cook until done. Package directions are good guides for the preparation of rice and pastas. Doneness can be checked by mashing a small sample with a fork or by tasting. Next, add the sauce mix and, after blending, add freeze-dried or retort meats and dried vegetables. Remove the pot from the heat, cover, and allow to stand for about 5 minutes on a heat-resistant insulated surface (a wooden snow shovel works well). Serve.

Note: The main dish can be prepared at home, spread in a shallow pan, and frozen. (Prepare the dish with less water than usual so that water can be added on the trail.) To use the frozen dish on the trail, break the frozen food into smaller pieces and add it to hot water.

Preparation of rice depends upon the type used. Uncooked rice can be started in boiling or in warm water, brought to a boil, and covered. Polished rice cooks in about 20 minutes. Brown rice takes about 40 minutes. Instant rice, which needs only to be rehydrated, is added to boiling water, then removed from the heat. Some seasoned rice mixes are browned in butter prior to adding water.

The starch in your evening meal could be instant mashed potatoes. To prepare, simply follow package directions.

Many varieties of cooked desserts can be prepared for winter camping. Those calling for preparation in the refrigerator are especially appropriate for camping below 38°F. Puddings, cheesecake, and gelatin desserts are all good and can be enhanced with a warm sauce.

Cold-Weather Food Preparation Tips

- Use stainless steel containers for cooking whenever possible. They are easy to cook with and to clean.
- Use insulated plastic cups, bowls, and spoons, if possible. Wooden cups and spoons are also good for winter camping as there is much less heat loss than with metal.
- A small camp stove is usually a great help.
- Rice is one of the best items in your "cupboard" for any camp menu. It can be used in many different ways for main dishes, breakfasts, or desserts, takes a small amount of space, and is easily prepared.
- Fats are important in the winter to release heat and energy slowly. A good source of vegetable fat is corn oil margarine, which can be used in almost anything. Fats give energy of about 9 calories per gram, compared to carbohydrates and protein, which yield about 4 per gram.
- In provisioning for winter camping, use 40 percent carbohydrates, 20 percent protein, and 40 percent fats. This is not a hard-and-fast rule, but a guide in choosing your foods. Half of the protein should be from high-quality proteins: milk, meat, and eggs.
- Substituting caffeine-free coffee or tea for those containing caffeine helps to combat dehydration and prevent headache.
- When making trail biscuits, use whole-wheat flour, which provides more protein, nutrients, and fiber than white flour.
- Peanut butter and honey make a very good spread. Mix them together at home and package the mixture in individual servings.

Cooking Equipment

These stoves work well with a 3- or 4-quart pot. The only utensils needed for a group of three to four are the pots, a couple of cooking spoons, and a cup, bowl, and spoon for each member of the group.

An alcohol stove and cooking set. These cooksets are excellent for groups of three to four people in cold-weather camping.

Coleman Peak I stove set on an insulating cover

Cookset for three or four persons

An alcohol stove used in cold weather camping, set on a wooden snow scoop for insulation

Cooking on a Coleman Peak I stove using a BSA Trail Oven

Water Collection

Several methods can be used to collect and heat water on the trail. However, it is important to remember that all water collected must be purified before use.

The Water Machine

This is a simple method to get liquid water from snow.

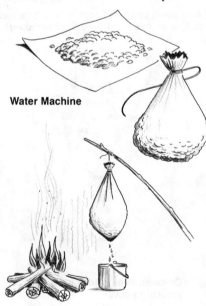

Water Machine

- Use a clean piece of cloth, such as an old bedsheet, that will let water through. The cloth should be 4 to 5 feet square.
- Pile snow in the middle, and tie the sheet like a bag of laundry.
- Hang the bag about 3 feet from the fire.
- Catch the water as it drips from the bag.
- Purify the water before using it.

Water Bottle

Use a wide-necked plastic pint jar or vinyl pouch. The plastic jars in which jam, jelly, or ice cream toppings are purchased work well. In the Okpik program, we also use a wide-necked vinyl pouch in which snow can be placed.

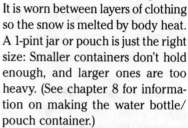

It is worn between layers of clothing so the snow is melted by body heat. A 1-pint jar or pouch is just the right size: Smaller containers don't hold enough, and larger ones are too heavy. (See chapter 8 for information on making the water bottle/pouch container.)

Remember to wear the water bottle between the layers of clothing so that the bottle stays warm. Take the bottle to bed with you at night. This allows you to have a drink during the night if you get thirsty, and provides water to start breakfast in the morning.

Water Bottle

Water bottle slung from neck and held next to body to prevent freezing.

45

The Finnish Marshmallow

This is a simple way to get a small amount of water in a hurry.

- In an area with packed or crusty snow, cut a block of snow with your snow knife.
- Suspend the block from a stick.
- Hold it close to the flame.
- Catch the water in a cup or other container.
- Purify the water before using it.

Note: Since snow shrinks when melting, the "marshmallow" will stay on the stick as long as it is not too close to the fire.

Finnish Marshmallow

The Latrine

Essential to the comfort and welfare of any camp is the location and construction of the outdoor toilet. The ideal toilet is a sheltered nook in the underbrush, close to camp, that provides sufficient privacy. Two trees about 10 inches in diameter and 3 to 4 feet apart make a sturdy base. Stomp down the snow between the trees, and then remove any leaves, twigs or moss that can be set to one side. Save these to cover the site when camp is abandoned.

Lash two smooth, sturdy poles about 3 inches in diameter between the two trees, on opposite sides. Adjust the lower one to the appropriate height for a seat; tie the other one higher for use as a backrest. Skilled latrine-builders are not easy to come by, so one who can speedily lash up a good facility is awarded an honored place in the group. Some campers leave a roll of paper at the latrine, stuffed inside an empty 2-pound coffee can or some other container. However, squirrels have a habit of gnawing holes in toilet paper, with dismaying results. Instead, keep your paper bagged in plastic at the campsite, and take a roll out to the latrine when needed.

When you break camp, untie the poles, remove the rope, cover the site between the trees with the duff and moss removed earlier, and then sprinkle a covering of snow over the site. It is best to take the used paper back to camp and burn it in the fire, though some put a match to it right at the latrine. Although human wastes disintegrate rapidly through bacterial and plant activity once warm weather comes, toilet paper does not degrade as fast, although it eventually will. If used toilet paper is not burned, anchor it down so that it does not get blown about the campsite. If you don't burn it, cover it with a layer of turf and twigs under a snow cover.

If there is no snow, use the techniques described in Trail and Camp Sanitation, appendix E.

A tarp can also be used for privacy.

Outdoor Latrine in Snow Country

Chapter 5

First Aid

All leaders should complete a basic first aid course before taking a group camping in cold weather. A good group first aid kit is necessary, and individual kits for each camper should be encouraged. The best references for cold-weather first aid are the same as for mild-weather activities, with the addition of specialty manuals that cover cold-weather injuries, such as the two by Dr. William Forgey and the one by E. Russel Kodet and Bradford Angier that are listed in the bibliography.

The group first aid kit is important. Use references suited for the group, the area, and climate where you camp to aid you in selecting a first aid kit. BSA manuals that address first aid (*The Official Scoutmaster Handbook*, the *Fieldbook*, and the *First Aid* merit badge pamphlet) are all excellent choices. The manuals by Dr. Forgey have appropriate suggestions for group kits, as does the book by Russel Kodet and Bradford Angier.

This chapter is not a first aid course, but an explanation of some common cold-weather problems. Prevention of injury is an important consideration in cold-weather camping. Repeated reference is made to dehydration precautions, since dehydration can be a serious problem in cold weather. Drinking plenty of liquids is important at all times, but even more so in the cold. Without proper water intake, neither the food you eat nor your body fat can be used for warmth or energy. You need at least 2 to 3 quarts of water each day to metabolize food and stored energy. Wearing a 1-pint water bottle around your neck is a good way to keep water available.

Dehydration

Dehydration is a condition that results from excessive loss of body water, either from too little intake, too much output, or a combination of both. Water is taken into the body through the mouth and is absorbed from the gastrointestinal tract. It is lost through the lungs, skin, gastrointestinal tract, and the kidneys. Exposure to cold has a diuretic effect that results in an increased output of urine. This helps to explain why medical records indicate that victims of cold injuries such as frostbite and hypothermia are usually dehydrated to some extent.

The maintenance of the body's water level depends on the regular intake of water. Under normal conditions water intake is regulated by the "thirst mechanism." In cold environments, however, the thirst mechanism is not a dependable indicator of body water needs.

With the onset of dehydration, one of the first things to happen is impairment of the ability to reason, making clear thinking difficult. For this reason, you may not realize you are thirsty or that you are not consuming enough liquids. Another effect of dehydration is that the color of the urine darkens. It is often easier to recognize a change in urine color than to judge liquid intake in cold weather. This makes urine color a more reliable guide to dehydration than thirst when cold-weather camping.

Prevention

In order to prevent dehydration:

- Individuals must be properly instructed on the need to drink at least 2 quarts of water a day (not including coffee).

- Fluid intake (water) should be increased at the first sign of changes in the color of the urine, i.e., darker yellow.

- In cold-weather survival situations, avoid dehydrating foods and fluids such as coffee or other drinks containing caffeine, and foods high in protein.

Symptoms

Body water deficiency of 1 to 5 percent of body weight results in the following conditions:

- Increased pulse rate
- Nausea and loss of appetite
- Dark urine color or constipation
- Irritability, fatigue, sleepiness
- Thirst (may not be noticeable in cold weather)

A body water deficiency of 6 to 10 percent of body weight results in the following conditions:

- Headache, dizziness
- Labored breathing
- Tingling in extremities
- Absence of salivation
- Inability to walk
- Cyanosis (bluish or grayish skin color)

A body water deficiency of 11 to 20 percent of body weight results in the following conditions:

- Swollen tongue, inability to swallow
- Dim vision, deafness
- Shriveled, numb skin
- Painful urination
- Delirium, unconsciousness, and death

Treatment

In mild cases of dehydration, the victim should drink liquids, keep warm, and get plenty of rest. More severe cases require professional medical treatment.

Prognosis

Remember, early detection and treatment should result in no disabling after-effects. Undetected and untreated cases of dehydration may result in severe cold-weather injuries such as hypothermia and frostbite. Mildly dehydrated

Natural Setting for Cold-Weather Injury

Windy →

← Cold

Wet →

← Tired

persons become careless and listless, and become unwilling or unable to maintain good hygienic and preventive measures. It is important to be alert to this possibility and reinforce use of the buddy system.

Hypothermia

Hypothermia is a lowering of the temperature of the inner core of the body that can and usually does happen above freezing, in the temperature range of 30°F (−1°C) to 50°F (10°C). The victim may not recognize the symptoms and may not be able to think clearly enough to counteract hypothermia. Injury or death may result.

Predisposing Conditions

The following factors make a person more susceptible to hypothermia:

- Poor physical condition
- Inadequate nutrition and water intake
- Thin build
- Nonprotective clothing
- Getting wet (even from drizzle or snow, not just rain)
- Inadequate protection from wind, rain, and snow
- Exhaustion

Symptoms

As with dehydration, one of the first problems is loss of ability to reason, and the victim may not recognize the symptoms. Due to various factors, the body's heat production cannot keep up with heat loss. As the body begins to cool at the skin surface, shivering occurs to release heat by increasing metabolism through contraction and relaxation of the muscles. Shivering may become intense, but as heat loss continues, it will cease. The body tries to protect the vital organs, and will cut off the blood supply to "nonessential" parts such as hands, arms, feet, and legs. As heat loss continues, body functions are progressively impaired, shivering stops, blood thickens, the heart is overtaxed, respiration may cease, and cardiac arrest may occur. This is sometimes described as freezing from the inside out. Signs of hypothermia that can be observed by others include:

- Slowing of pace, drowsiness, fatigue
- Stumbling
- Thickness of speech
- Amnesia
- Irrationality, poor judgment
- Hallucinations
- Loss of perceptual contact with environment
- Blueness of skin (cyanosis)
- Dilation (enlargement) of pupils
- Decreased heart and respiration rate
- Stupor

Self-Testing for Hypothermia

Test for hypothermia by touching the little finger and thumb together. If this cannot be done, stop immediately and warm up. Symptoms of hypothermia that can be felt or noticed by the victim include:

- Fatigue, drowsiness, exhaustion, unwillingness to go on
- Feeling of deep cold or numbness
- Poor coordination
- Stumbling

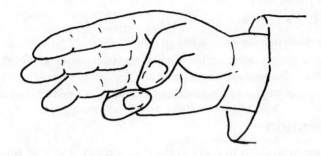

Testing for hypothermia

Anyone experiencing the following symptoms should seek help immediately:

- Poor articulation of words (thickness of speech)
- Disorientation
- Decrease in shivering followed by rigidity of muscles
- Blueness of skin (cyanosis)
- Slowness of pulse, irregular or weak pulse

Treatment

If the victim is unconscious, obtain and maintain an airway, check for pulse and respiration, and begin artificial respiration or CPR as needed. To reduce heat loss:

- Shelter the victim from wind and weather.
- Insulate the victim from the ground.
- Change wet clothing.
- Put on windproof, waterproof gear.
- Increase exercise, if possible.

To add heat:

- Put the victim in a prewarmed sleeping bag or blankets (a cold one will just rob more heat and add to the problem).
- Give hot drinks, followed by candy or other high-sugar foods (if conscious).

- Apply heat with hot stones or hot canteens of water. (Be careful not to burn the victim.)
- Huddle for body heat from others.
- Place someone in sleeping bag or blanket with the victim.
- Place victim in a tub of 105°F (40.6°C) water. Never go above 110°F (43.3°C), or you may injure the victim.
- After the victim is warm from soaking in the tub, dry the victim thoroughly.

Prevention

Use these procedures to guard against the dangers of hypothermia:

- Get plenty of rest and maintain good nutrition before and during cold-weather camping.
- Consume plenty of high-energy food (particularly sugars) and water while camping.
- Use waterproof and winterproof clothing, some of which should be wool.
- Carry emergency bivouac (camping and shelter) equipment.
- Make camp early in a storm, or if lost, injured, or tired.
- Exercise to keep up the body's heat function.
- Appoint an experienced person to watch the group for signs of hypothermia, and always adhere to the hypothermia watcher's decisions.
- Carry proper clothing, footgear, and emergency equipment.
- Take immediate corrective action for signs or symptoms of hypothermia.

Frostbite

Frostbite is tissue injury involving the actual freezing of skin and subcutaneous (underlying) tissues. Recovery from frostbite is slow, usually taking weeks or months. Severe frostbite may lead to gangrene and necessitate amputation of the affected parts. Once exposed, the patient will be predisposed toward frostbite in the future.

Frostbite occurs when the body needs heat elsewhere; it redirects blood flow from the extremities to protect internal organs. Capillary beds constrict; later they become damaged. The blood thickens and becomes sludge-like, and circulation slows. Ice crystals form in skin cells, drawing off moisture and dehydrating them. The skin can't get the oxygen, nutrients, and liquids it needs and can't eliminate wastes, further damaging the tissue. As exposure continues, freezing and damage go deeper in the skin until the full thickness, including the bone, freezes.

Predisposing Conditions

The following conditions make frostbite more likely:

- Prolonged exposure to temperatures 32°F (0°C) or below
- Brief exposure to extremely low temperatures—minus 25°F (−32°C) and below
- Wind, humidity, rain, or snow (exposed flesh can freeze in 15 seconds at −30°F (−35°C), with a 30 mph wind)
- Exposed body parts
- Restriction of circulation
- Fatigue, poor nutrition, poor liquid intake, and poor physical condition
- Previous case of frostbite or other cold injury

Symptoms

The symptoms of frostbite vary with its severity. First-degree frostbite, or frostnip, is the least severe form. Second-degree frostbite is superficial and causes no permanent damage. Third- and fourth-degree frostbite are quite severe; they result in permanent damage and may require amputation. The symptoms of each degree of frostbite follow:

First Degree (Frostnip)

- Warnings include redness, pain, burning, stinging, or prickly sensation.
- Following the early warning signs, pain disappears and there is a sudden blanching of the skin (it turns white, gray, or waxy looking).
- The skin may look mottled.
- Skin is firm to the touch but resilient underneath.
- On thawing, there is aching, pain, or brownness. The skin may peel off, and the part may remain cold for some time.

Second Degree (Superficial Frostbite, Frostbite)

- All signs and symptoms of first-degree frostbite can occur.

- No pain; the part may feel dead or "like a stump."
- Numbness; the part may be immobile or very hard to move.
- Tissue is hard to the touch, including underneath layers.
- After thawing (takes 3 to 20 days), pain, large blisters, sweating.
- Black or discolored skin sloughs off, leaving tender new skin.

Third Degree (Severe Frostbite)

- The full thickness of the skin is involved.
- After thawing, aching and throbbing continue for 2 to 5 weeks.

Fourth Degree (Severe Frostbite)

- The full thickness of skin and bone are frozen.
- Swelling and sweating occur in affected areas.
- Black, hard scabs form, surrounded by blisters that slough off, leaving ulcers which heal in about 60 days.
- After thawing, affected skin becomes black and shriveled or mummified.
- Gangrene may develop.
- Amputation may be necessary.

Treatment

Take the following steps to treat frostbite:

- Do not rub the affected area with snow. Hold it over fire, or use cold water to thaw it. (Note the warning, below, about thawing frostbitten limbs.)
- Exercise the affected area to promote blood circulation.
- Place victim's hands in armpits or crotch, blow warm air on victim's nose, place victim's foot inside your shirt against chest, etc.
- Make certain that insulation is adequate to prevent recurrence or further injury. Check for hypothermia.
- Cover the frostbitten area and insulate it to prevent further injury.
- **Do not** attempt to thaw frostbitten limbs in the field. It is less harmful for the victim to walk out on a frostbitten limb than to thaw it in the field. Thawing only risks additional injury and the victim will be in too much pain to walk. Check for hypothermia.

- Once the injury is thawed, the victim must be carried. However, if partial thawing occurs while walking, the victim should continue to walk out to avoid refreezing the part.

Once in camp headquarters or other suitable facility:
- Rewarm affected areas rapidly using water at about 105°F (41°C). Be certain the water does not exceed 110°F (43.3°C), or it may harm the victim.

- Thaw frozen boots, gloves, etc. while on the part, and then gently remove them or cut them away carefully.

- Gently wash the area with soap.

- Discontinue warming when the part becomes flushed.

- Dry the area thoroughly and gently.

- Place gauze pads or cotton between fingers and toes.

- Dress the entire part with suitable bandages.

- Provide bed rest and elevate the frostbitten part.

- Check for and treat hypothermia.

- Make certain the person is transported to a hospital or seen by a physician as soon as possible.

- Don't be overzealous in your application of heat. Test to make certain that 110°F (43.3°C) is not exceeded.

Prevention

The following precautions help reduce the risk of frostbite:
- Prevent heat loss with proper insulation—cover exposed skin.

- Guard against windchill and moisture. Dry clothing is 240 times better than wet clothing.

- Maintain good nutrition, drink water, keep a good metabolic rate, and maintain an adequate core temperature.

- Use buddy system to check face, nose, and ears for frostnip and frostbite.

- Periodically make faces, exercise ears with hands, keep feet and hands moving.

- Don't wear restrictive clothing. Dress in layers.

- Remember—when the pain goes away, you are in danger of severe injury from frostbite. If you haven't corrected the problem by then, you are in trouble and need to correct it immediately.

Chilblains

A chilblain is a lesion that has been described as trench foot of the hand, although it may also occur on the lower extremity or the ears. Chilblains may disappear within a few days, or may assume a chronic form and last for weeks or months. In the chronic form, the condition is also known as erythrocyanosis, Basin's disease, lupus, pernio, and dermatitis hiemalis.

Chilblains are provoked by cold above freezing temperatures that is experienced intermittently over long periods of time. It is observed chiefly in climates characterized by moderate cold and a high degree of humidity. The subjects are usually young persons whose hands are likely to be colder than normal. The majority of victims have a history of daily exposure in a cold, moist atmosphere. Usually, an injury of the preceding day has not been allowed to heal before added exposure on the next day. Thus, one lesion tends to develop over another.

Symptoms

A typical chilblain first appears as a red, swollen, tender lesion, which is usually warm or hot to the touch. The only symptom at this time is itching. When the lesion becomes chronic, swelling may increase and the tissue becomes tender. The color becomes a deep or reddish purple. Blister formation and ulceration may develop. In the chronic form, itching is replaced by tenderness and actual pain.

Other Damp-Foot Injuries

Trench foot, or immersion foot, is a disease of the sympathetic nerves and blood vessels of the feet resulting from prolonged exposure to cold and wet environments. These injuries do not require freezing temperatures. Partial causes include immobility of the limbs with legs and feet down, as when sitting or standing; insufficient clothing; and constriction of parts of the body by boots, socks, and other garments.

Symptoms

The immediate symptoms include numbness and tingling pain with itching. These progress to leg cramps and complete numbness. The skin initially appears reddened and later becomes progressively pale and mottled and then gray or blue.

Prevention

Take the following precautions:

- Keep feet dry by wearing waterproof footgear and by keeping the floors of the shelter dry.

- Clean and dry socks and boots daily.

- Dry feet as soon as possible after getting them wet. Warm them with your hands. Apply foot powder and put on dry socks.

- If it is necessary to wear wet boots and socks, continually exercise your feet by wiggling your toes and bending your ankles. Never wear tight boots.

Treatment

Handle the feet gently. They should not be rubbed or massaged. If necessary, cleanse them carefully with plain white soap and water, dry, elevate, and leave them exposed. While it is desirable to warm the patient, the feet should always be kept at room temperature. The victim should be carried and not permitted to walk.

Snow Blindness

Snow blindness is an inflammation of the eye caused by exposure to reflected ultraviolet rays when the sun is shining brightly on an expanse of snow. It is particularly likely to occur after the fall of new snow, even when the rays of the sun are partially obscured by a light mist or fog. The risk is also increased at high altitudes.

Symptoms and Treatment

Symptoms of snow blindness are a sensation of grit in the eyes (made worse by eyeball movement), watering, redness, headache, and increased pain on exposure to light. First aid measures consist of blindfolding and rest. If further exposure to light is unavoidable, the eyes should be protected with dark bandages or the darkest available sunglasses. The condition heals in a few days without permanent damage, once unprotected exposure to sunlight is stopped.

Prevention

In most cases, snow blindness is due to negligence or failure to wear sunglasses. Do not wait for discomfort to develop before putting on glasses. Your eyes may already have been deeply burned by the time any pain is felt. Putting on sunglasses is essential to prevent further injury, but damage has already been done.

Carbon Monoxide Poisoning

Carbon monoxide poisoning is a constant threat during cold-weather camping. Carbon monoxide is created by incomplete combustion of fuel due to insufficient air supply. Carbon monoxide is odorless, colorless, and tasteless; it can kill instantly.

Symptoms and Treatment

The first symptom of carbon monoxide poisoning is a tightness across the forehead, followed by a headache and pounding of the heart. Weakness and unconsciousness follow in a very short time. Fresh air, oxygen, warmth, and rest are treatments for carbon monoxide poisoning. Artificial respiration may be a lifesaver.

Prevention

All heated shelters, particularly vehicles with personal heaters, provide the potential for carbon monoxide poisoning. All heated shelters and vehicles must be ventilated. Windows and doors must be left open to permit entry of fresh air, regardless of the outdoor temperature.

Remember: Never use flames in tents or in airtight enclosures.

Chapter 6

Shelters

Shelters are an important consideration in planning for any type of cold weather outing. Your first winter campout should be in a cabin or other fixed shelter. The next time you may want to try a tent, or if in snow country, a "thermal" or snow shelter. You should even consider shelters for cold-weather hikes. Crew equipment, different from that used in mild-weather camping, must also be considered.

Types of Shelters

You can choose from a variety of shelters when you go winter camping. Possiblities include cabins, tents, thermal shelters, and other natural shelters.

Cabins

Your first cold-weather camping should be done at a camp or other location where cabins are available. A cabin can be small or quite large, like the lodge of many camps. The size is not the important consideration. The important part is how it helps you train for more extensive cold-weather camping. The Okpik sleeping cabin (with front and rear doors) designed by the BSA Engineering Service is available for use where small cabins are needed.

Tents

Many types and styles of tents are available. The BSA Supply Service is a good resource for tentage. Most styles of tents work in cold weather. You may want one a little larger than the one you use in the summer, since cold-weather clothing and bedding take up more room. Your tent should be large enough to that you can sit up in it.

If you camp in the mountains, you may prefer a mountaineering tent. A tent design that works well for cold-weather snow camping is the "A" style tent. This tent is a BSA design made by the National Supply Division and developed by the Northern Tier National High Adventure Program as a year-round tent. It can be used with a self-supporting frame. The double entrances work well for weather protection and make zippers unnecessary. The tent will usually accommodate four campers, is large enough to dress in, and is spacious enough for extra equipment. The tunnel doors can also be used for storage. A vestibule can be attached to either end, extending the storage available. A frost liner can be constructed to fit the inside of the tent to provide more insulation. This also helps to keep the tent frost-free in extreme low temperatures.

"A"-style tent with tunnel entrance on both ends

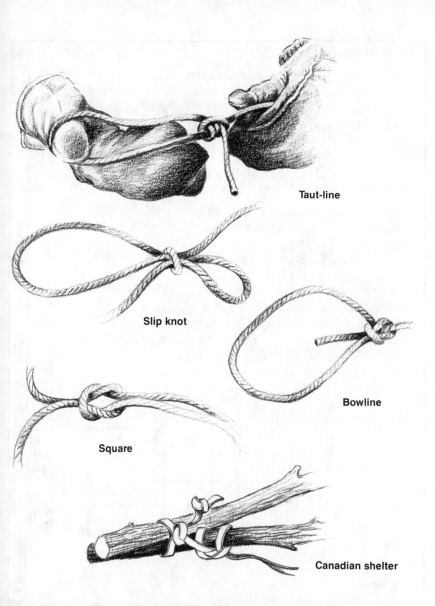

Taut-line

Slip knot

Bowline

Square

Canadian shelter

Knots to Use in Cold-Weather Camping

The Canadian shelter knot can take the place of lashing in cold weather. It is really nothing more than two overhand knots, finished with a couple of half hitches. It is generally tied using the outer cover of the nylon 550 cord.

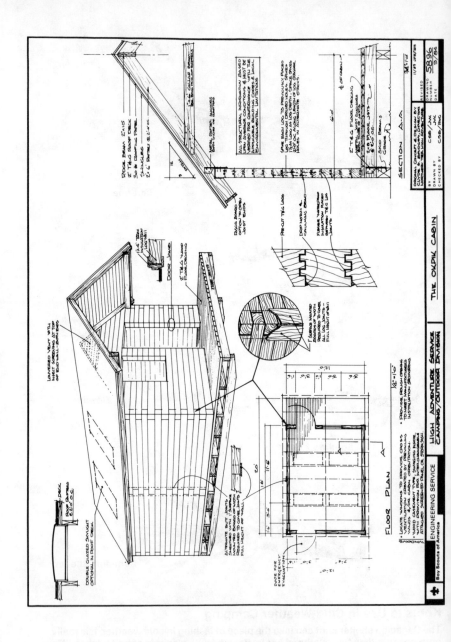

BSA drawing from Engineering Service—No. 5896—The Okpik Cabin

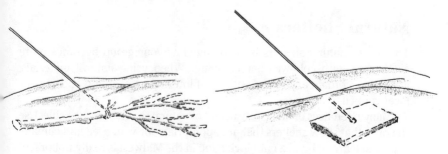

Two methods of holding down the tent ropes in the snow

Some North American Indians used a form of frost liner, usually referred to as a dew cloth, in their shelters. A frost liner for a tent is nothing more than a lightweight inner tent. It can be made of almost any lightweight, porous material—worn bed sheeting works very well. It should be suspended inside the tent with about 2 inches of space between it and the tent walls. The frost liner provides insulation and protection from wind, helping hold heat in a smaller area, less affected by air currents. The warm, moist air inside the frost liner passes through the porous material and forms frost on the outside of the liner.

Each morning, the frost liner can be taken out and the frost removed. It should be packed separately from the tent, dried as often as practical, and replaced inside the tent every evening.

CAUTION: Open flames should not be used in any tent. Refer to appendix B for the BSA policy on the use of stoves and fuels.

BSA Tunnel Tent

Natural Shelters

The use of natural shelters is encouraged as your group becomes more acquainted with cold-weather camping. When using natural materials, do so in accordance with the policies of low-impact camping and of your local council.

Many references on the construction of natural shelters are available. Use the ones that show shelters that are appropriate for your area and climate. Trying to learn to build a cut-block igloo in the Midwest is really not practical since you do not have the packed, windblown snow required.

Snow shelters, except in the mountains and the high Arctic, are usually of the snow dome-type called quinzees. The thermal shelters shown in this handbook are good in almost any area where there is snow.

Cold weather demands a tighter closing of structures than mild weather does. This necessitates more attention to proper ventilation. Review the liquid fuel policy as well as the policy in your local area regarding the use of natural materials before you consider means for staying warm. Carbon monoxide is a product of inefficient burning of fossil fuels. It is colorless and odorless, and can be deadly. Carbon monoxide is a threat in any camp, but is a greater problem in cold weather.

This shelter is constructed of a framework covered by fabric and then either boughs or straw. The shelter is finished by piling loose snow over the framework. Notice that the doorway has been identified. This will be closed with the same style of closure as used with the other snow shelters. A vent will be placed in the side of the shelter.

Thermal Shelters

A thermal shelter is any natural shelter that, through insulation, uses the heat coming from the earth to warm it. In temperate climates the earth is continually giving off 12° to 16°F of heat. This doesn't sound very warm, since you know that 32°F (0°C) is freezing, but it makes a difference when the air temperature is well below freezing, or even below zero.

With a good, insulated thermal shelter at −20°F (−6.6°C), the heat of the earth combined with the body heat of two people warms the shelter to around the freezing point. That is a difference of 52°F (11.1°C) from the temperature outside!

A shelter can be large, or small enough to accommodate one person in emergency or survival situations. The following are several important points about the thermal shelter:

- A door plug must be used, or any heat trapped is immediately lost.

- Each sleeper needs an insulating pad underneath his body. Even though the earth is giving off heat, it is still much colder than your body temperature. Unprotected, your body loses heat to the earth by conduction.

- Ventilation holes should be made at a 45° angle in the side of the shelter. Since warm, moist air passes though these vents, it is necessary to continually clear them of frost.

- Make the shelter so that you can sit up without touching the ceiling.

- The more insulating snow that is piled on the shelter, the warmer it will be.

- Do not, under any circumstances, use an open flame in a thermal shelter.

Building Snow Shelters

The snow shelters described in this handbook are the cut-block igloo, the molded snow dome called the *quinzee,* and the popular T-shaped snow cave. Several other shelters are described in the manuals listed as references for this chapter.

Patience and practice are both necessary to develop skill at building any type of snow shelter. If you are in the mountains, expert instruction is suggested. The mountains have additional hazards that go well beyond the scope of this guide. Avalanches and extreme temperature fluctuations are just two of the serious mountain conditions that necessitate competent, skilled instruction.

Snow shelters hold a certain fascination for Scouts, and since they are easy to construct, you will find they work very well. Even in extremely low temperatures, snow-shelter builders usually get wet. Therefore, certain precautions should be taken. In a moist snow shelter, drying clothes is difficult. Follow these guidelines when building a thermal shelter:

- Pace the work on the shelter—let everyone get involved. Stop before perspiration becomes a problem. Remember to ventilate.

- Proceed slower than you think you should to avoid overheating.

- Scouts in the Scandinavian countries use a clothing item called a *fotposer* to keep legs and feet dry. The fotposer is just a large, waterproof sock that covers the boot and continues up the leg, fastening like a pair of chaps. Chapter 8 shows how to make them. Another Scandinavian Scout item used in shelter building, the *vindsekk,* or wind sock, is a small, portable shelter that provides protection when building a shelter. The vindsekk has several other uses, and its construction is also explained in chapter 8.

- Try to keep mitts from getting wet.

- Watch out for snow on garments. Continue to use the buddy system and keep snow brushed off.

- Relax! You are not building a lasting monument. Snow shelters do not survive when warm weather returns.

The first time a group builds a snow shelter should be while camping in a cabin or tent. Learn how first, then use the skills to build shelters in which you will actually sleep.

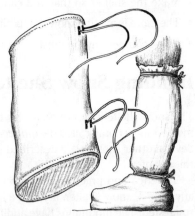

Fotposer—**A waterproof foot and leg covering that is helpful in keeping the lower leg dry when building snow shelters.**

The temperatures in a well-constructed snow shelter will rarely be below freezing when campers are inside. If you leave the door wide open with no closure, the shelter will be the same temperature as the outside air. Ventilation is important in a snow shelter. The vent holes should be at a 45-degree angle. If you place them in the center of the roof, the holes will get larger as the warm air rushes out. Placed at a 45 degree angle in the side of the dome, the vent replaces the slightly cooled air without causing a draft in the shelter.

When planning to construct any type of snow shelter, the following points must be considered:

- Never plan to build or stay in a snow shelter if the temperature is above freezing. Snow provides excellent insulation in below-freezing conditions, but it is cold and wet when temperatures are above freezing.

- Always let the snow set at least 1 to 2 hours before starting to dig when constructing a snow dome or quinzee.

- Use the buddy system during snow shelter construction. It is important to have good supervision outside the structure, along with extra scoops and shovels in case of a cave-in.

- An arched roof is a key factor in snow shelter construction. Make sure everyone understands this principle.

- When constructing snow caves in mountainous areas, consult a specialist regarding the proper location for constructing caves.

- When sleeping in a snow shelter, be sure to keep digging tools inside in case an unexpected exit is necessary.

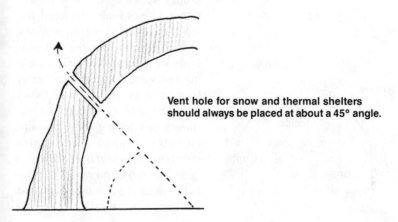

**Vent hole for snow and thermal shelters
should always be placed at about a 45° angle.**

Igloos

One of the most primitive and most effective shelters ever used by people is the snow house, or *igloo*, used by the Inuit for centuries. The igloo has endured because of its efficient and simple structural form, ease of construction, and excellent protection from the winter elements. It has been estimated that if properly constructed, the igloo will maintain an inside temperature up to 100 degrees above the −40°F (−40°C) temperatures prevalent in the Arctic.

Considerations for the proper construction of an igloo include size, materials, protection from wind, and wall construction.

Size. The diameter of a snow house or igloo should not exceed 10 feet. A diameter of more than 10 feet would require a theoretically perfect dome construction that is virtually impossible to construct in the field.

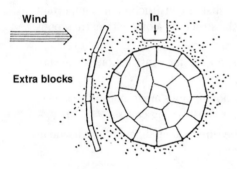

Materials. The igloo is built from blocks of snow cut from the depth where your feet stop sinking. The top layers of dry powder are not satisfactory. You will need a knife or saw blade 14 to 20 inches long, a cord at least the length of the radius of the igloo, and waterproof gloves or mittens.

Protection from Wind. Since for proper ventilation, the igloo entrance is never sealed or closed, the top of the entrance should be about 18 inches lower than the bed platform to prevent the warmed air from escaping. The entrance should be located so that the wind blows past the opening and does not pile snow into it. Strong winds containing airborne snow and ice particles could cut through at the base of the igloo. This can be prevented by placing extra blocks of snow at the base on the windward side.

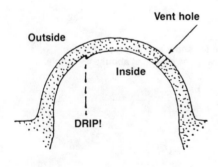

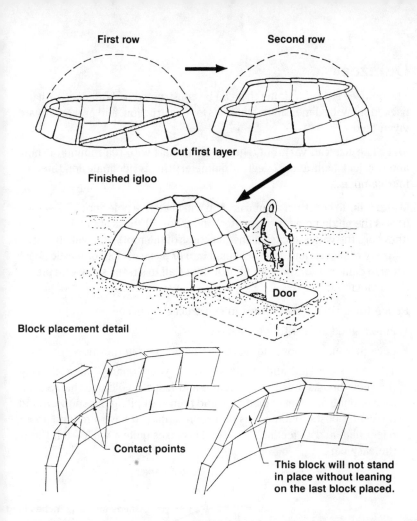

First row

Second row

Cut first layer

Finished igloo

Door

Block placement detail

Contact points

This block will not stand in place without leaning on the last block placed.

Wall Construction. The wall is made of 8-inch-thick snow blocks with sides of 18 and 30 inches. Snow blocks may be replaced with slabs of clear lake ice for a window effect, if the ice is available. The first layer should be cut as illustrated to start the wall spiral for the dome shape. If building on a slope, set up a level course before starting the spiral course. Proper thickness of the walls is important. If they are too thick, the collected heat inside will cause melting, and if they are too thin, frost forms on the inside surface. Also, any projection on the inside surface will form a point of dripping, which can be corrected by smoothing out the spot. By keeping the interior surface smooth, water will run down within the wall rather than dripping inside.

Quinzees

The quinzee is a snow dome that can be constructed without deep or hard-packed snow. Its dimensions, materials for construction, and procedures are given below.

Size. The size can vary, but a good size to start with is a mound of snow about 6 feet high and 12 feet in diameter; this is adequate for three or four campers.

Materials. To construct a quinzee, you will need one pole about 8 feet long (this is the guide pole for the center) and 30 or 40 sticks about 1 foot long (these are the gauge sticks for the thickness of the roof). You will also need a variety of shovels and snow scoops, a tarp or piece of cloth or plastic about 5 feet in diameter for the door plug, a stout staff to stir the snow, and plenty of warm clothing.

Procedure. Follow these steps to construct a quinzee:

- Find a good area with lots of snow.
- Lay out your location and place the center pole in the snow.
- Take the stout staff and stir the snow in your "quarry" area. Stirring the snow breaks down the structure and helps it hold together. Stir an area about 6 or 8 feet in diameter, and then start piling this snow around the center post. Continue this procedure until you have a mound about 6 feet high and 12 feet in diameter. This takes quite a while—but this is the easy part.

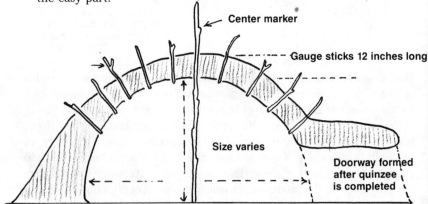

Building a quinzee: center pole and gauge sticks.

Building the quinzee: Shelter almost finished, still showing gauge sticks.

- Let the mound settle. This usually takes an hour or two.

- After the mound is settled, carefully put in your gauge sticks.

- Now comes the moment of truth. You start to dig out the entrance. A 24-inch hole is just about right. If the entrance remains firm, continue to scoop out the inside, using the gauge sticks to keep the thickness to 1 foot. Change diggers often to avoid overheating.

- Pile the excavated snow around the entrance to form a windbreak. Make a door plug (just like the water machine bag, chapter 4) and place it near the door.

- When you have finished the inside, be sure to make vents (usually two or three work best). Let the shelter stay open so the snow will harden.

- After the shelter is hardened, you can move in.

Building a quinzee: Finished shelter.

T-shaped Snow Cave

Snow caves are comfortable and practical winter shelters, eliminating the need for carrying a tent. They are not complicated to construct, and allow the builders an opportunity to improve while developing their burrowing skills. Snow caves, when all is said (and done) can be fun! However, the traditional, or conventional, snow cave has these critical limitations:

- The people digging the cave usually get wet, either from the snow or from perspiration.
- Only one person can dig; everyone else just waits.
- The cave takes a great deal of time, usually at least 2 hours, to build.

The T-shaped snow cave has these advantages:

- It is completed quickly because snow is excavated directly out a side wall, and digging is in the excavator's normal range of motion. A two-person cave can be completed in half an hour.
- The builders have less contact with the snow and expend less energy, and therefore stay drier than with standard snow cave construction.
- More efficient use is made of everyone. Every member of the group is active, and is protected from the weather sooner. Once inside the cave, the occupants can, as before, make the house into a home.

Procedure. When a snow bank is selected, the first camper starts by digging a rectangular entrance platform measuring about 18 inches wide by 5 feet high, extending about 3 feet into the bank. Next, dig a waist-high platform about 4 feet wide centered on the entrance platform. Develop this into a slot 18 inches high and 4 feet wide, extending into the bank. It is through this opening that snow from the enlargement process passes out, thereby eliminating the need for a second person to haul snow. The second person can be cutting or otherwise forming blocks or snowballs to later seal the front portion of the rectangular opening. (Snow excavated from the cave interior can be used.)

Continue to dig from the entrance platform in a standing or kneeling position, expanding the room in all directions (except down), and evacuating the snow through the rectangle. The waist-high platform becomes the floor of the cave. After excavating everything within easy reach, extend the entrance about 2 feet or so into the floor area and about 1 foot downward. Enter the partially constructed shelter: You should almost be able to stand. Continue to excavate out of the wind at that point.

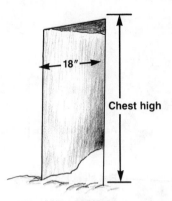

18″

Chest high

Dig the entrance tunnel 18 inches wide and chest high.

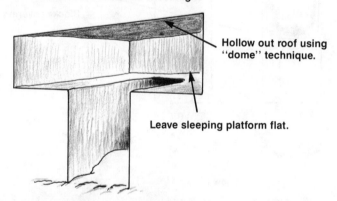

Hollow out roof using "dome" technique.

Leave sleeping platform flat.

Remove a rectangular portion of snow crosswise to the entrance. Then dig upward and in all directions—leaving the sleeping floor flat.

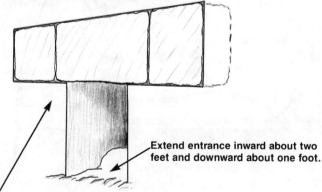

Extend entrance inward about two feet and downward about one foot.

Cut entrance blocks and place them across the entrance.

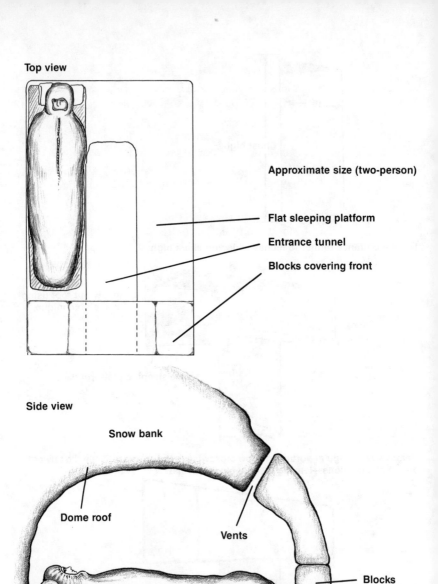

Top view

Approximate size (two-person)

Flat sleeping platform

Entrance tunnel

Blocks covering front

Side view

Snow bank

Dome roof

Vents

Blocks

Entrance

Door plug
as used with
quinzee

Completed two-person snow cave (cutaway view)

When the first camper has excavated enough to be able to sit on the floor, the second can enter. Continue to expand the cave moderately in all directions until the overall inside dimensions are about 7 feet long, 5 feet wide, and 3½ feet high.

When the interior is near completion, one camper fills in the sides of the horizontal slot with the snowblocks or snowballs previously constructed. One large block, or two smaller ones leaning against each other, will usually be sufficient to support the upper half of the entrance tunnel. After caulking any remaining holes, the shelter is finished.

When trying this technique for the first time, follow the recommended dimensions closely. It is best not to dig the entrance too far into the bank, but only far enough to be able to enter into a solidly roofed room. However, the depth of the snow, the slope, and various other terrain features may dictate modifications.

Equipment for Building and Maintaining Shelters

A few tools are necessary when camping in a snow-covered area that are not needed during mild weather or wet-cold conditions. These include a snow shovel or scoop, snow saw, snow knife, ice auger, whisk broom, and *anaotark* (see chapter 8).

If your group builds shelters, several snow shovels are essential. You can use almost any type of scoop or snow shovel, but be sure to include a few short mountaineering shovels for finishing the inside of a shelter. The wooden scoop described in chapter 8 is appropriate, and making it is an easy individual project. Each camper will then have a scoop that will move lots of snow.

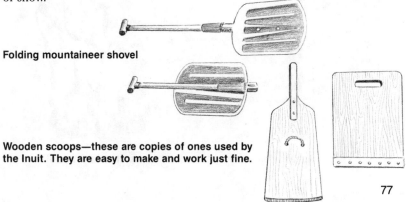

Folding mountaineer shovel

Wooden scoops—these are copies of ones used by the Inuit. They are easy to make and work just fine.

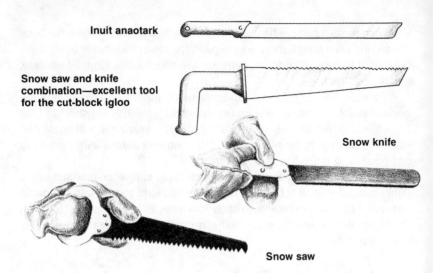

Inuit anaotark

Snow saw and knife combination—excellent tool for the cut-block igloo

Snow knife

Snow saw

The snow saw and the snow knife are used to build cut-block snow shelters.

An auger is necessary if you want to fish in a pond or lake. It is safer and easier to use than an ice spud or chisel. Check with a local fisherman to find out what style is best for your area.

Auger

Ice chisel or "spud"

An anaotark is an Inuit tool used to remove snow from clothing and equipment before entering a shelter. Each camper should have a personal snow removal tool, and use it every time a shelter is entered.

Tools for Building Snow Shelters

Chapter 7

Travel Techniques

Traveling in cold weather is the same as in other times of the year, unless there is freezing rain or snow. Proper planning is essential to get the most out of any trip, but there are several things to consider when planning to travel in cold weather. These are:

- Equipment, food, and clothing will be heavier than for most camping.
- Packs and other gear worn on the outside of jackets will have to be sized differently.
- Significantly more energy will be used in carrying the extra weight.
- There are fewer daylight hours.
- Temperature extremes can be dangerous. Temperatures are often above freezing in the late afternoon, but below freezing in the morning. Items left out at night will be frozen and must be thawed before use.
- Travel on the water, as on a canoe trip, may not be safe since the water temperature may be too low.

Backpacking

Cold-weather backpacking is covered in many manuals and specialty publications. Use BSA manuals and other backpacking literature for equipment and techniques to use in cold weather. Your group members should be experienced mild-weather backpackers: Cold-weather backpacking is not a good place for the novice to start. Day hikes with a minimum of equipment will give a good indication of how your group will fare on a cold-weather backpacking trip.

Be sure to have a good plan of action before starting on an overnight cold-weather trip. Since you will be carrying more weight and using more energy, don't plan to travel as far as you would during mild weather. Make sure you make camp early and that your shelter is well prepared for the night.

Traveling Over Snow

Travel where there is snow on the ground will either be on snowshoes or on skis. Backpacking can be more difficult when using snowshoes or skis, though the snow can be a benefit as well as a hindrance because it acts as insulation in certain circumstances. An alternative to backpacking is to pull a sled that has your gear on it.

Snow camping should be learned one step at a time. Your group's first snow outing should be a hike. A one-night campout will usually be the next step. The national high-adventure bases and several council camps offer excellent instruction in the basics of cold-weather camping. These programs are a good way to learn the techniques necessary for a successful trip. Experience is the key to good cold-weather camping, but it must be acquired gradually and thoroughly.

Snowshoeing

Snowshoeing is a great way to get out and see the back country. A lot of instruction isn't necessary, since it is relatively easy to learn. Look for books on the subject that will acquaint you with snowshoe equipment and basic techniques.

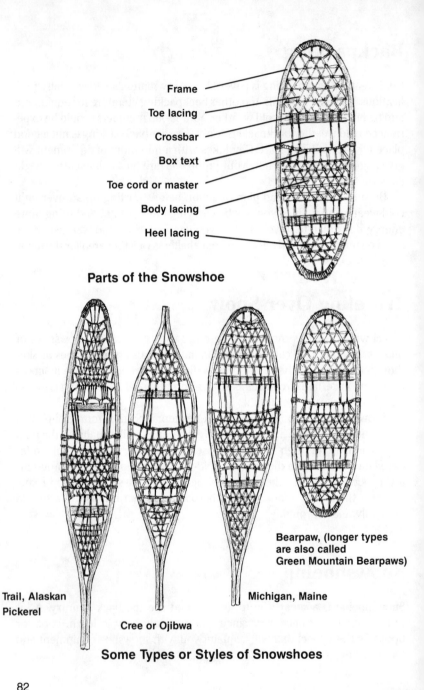

Frame
Toe lacing
Crossbar
Box text
Toe cord or master
Body lacing
Heel lacing

Parts of the Snowshoe

Bearpaw, (longer types
are also called
Green Mountain Bearpaws)

Trail, Alaskan
Pickerel

Michigan, Maine

Cree or Ojibwa

Some Types or Styles of Snowshoes

As you begin to snowshoe, you will notice that different muscles are used than for hiking. Familiarize yourself with snowshoes by taking a few short hikes. This should be done without a pack and with proper clothing for the weather. One of the first things you notice when snowshoeing is how much energy you use. Don't forget that when you use this energy, you need to keep drinking plenty of water. It is also necessary to ventilate properly, or perspiration will wet your inner clothing. Slow down; don't overheat. Pace yourself and keep up a steady, but not difficult, walk.

If the snow is very deep, you have to "break trail." This can be very difficult and takes a lot of energy. If you are by yourself, just take your time. If you are in a group, alternate trail-breaking often, even as frequently as every 2 or 3 minutes in deep snow. To alternate, the person breaking trail just steps to the side and the next one in line moves up. The trail breaker rests a minute and then falls in at the end of the line.

When snowshoeing, always walk in single file. This packs down the trail and makes traveling easier. If you return the next day over the same trail, it may have frozen hard enough that you will not even need your snowshoes.

There are many opinions as to what types of snowshoes and bindings are best. Ask a person familiar with snowshoeing to tell you what type of shoe and binding works best in your area. Many areas have snowshoe clubs that can provide you with information. An excellent way to become familiar with snowshoes is to make your own. Kits and instructions are available.

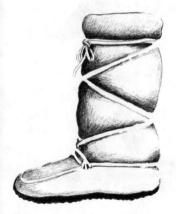

Steger-style mukluks

Mukluks being used on snowshoes. The binding is a firm toe piece with an elastic band (inner tube, bungee cord, etc.) behind the heel.

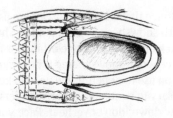
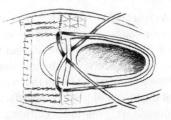

The emergency hitch, or "lampwick hitch," is an excellent snowshoe binding. It can be used with any style snowshoe and any style boot. This is a must-know for emergencies. A modification of this style of binding can also be used as an emergency binding for skis. This is done by looping the cord around a broken ski binding.

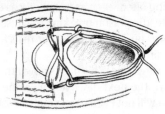
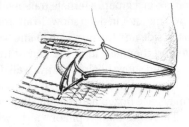

Emergency hitch ("lampwick hitch")

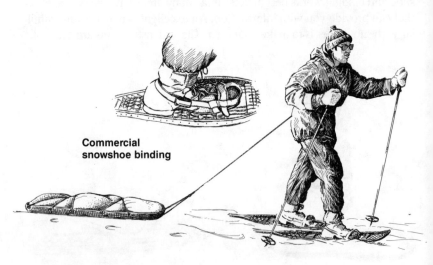

Commercial snowshoe binding

Skiing

It will take some instruction and practice before you and your group are competent enough to use cross-country or touring skis on a camping trip. Skiing instruction is available almost anywhere there is snow. Instructors enjoy teaching others the sport and are usually very helpful to Scout groups.

Many manuals are available for beginning skiers. The ones we suggest have proven reliable for Scouts in the Okpik program for several years. They provide accurate information on learning the techniques of ski camping. The *Fieldbook* is a good resource for the beginner. *Complete Cross-Country Skiing and Ski Touring* by William J. Lederer and Joe Pete Wilson is excellent. It has instructions on how to learn to ski in 60 minutes. It will take longer than that to become a ski-camper, but the book will help you get started.

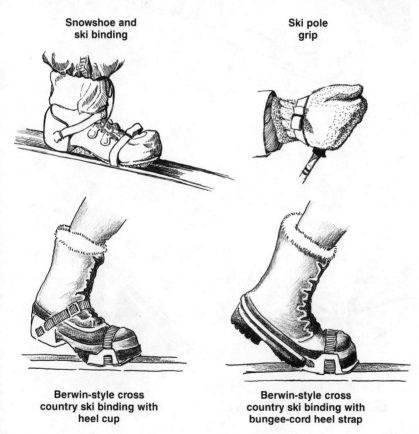

Snowshoe and ski binding

Ski pole grip

Berwin-style cross country ski binding with heel cup

Berwin-style cross country ski binding with bungee-cord heel strap

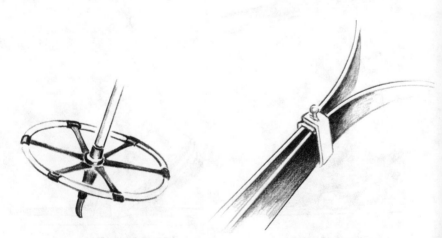

Deep snow baskets for ski poles

Ties to keep skis together

Pulling a Sled

The most efficient way to move your camp equipment in snow is with a sled. Carrying something on your back will never be as efficient as letting the snow help you support and slide it along. It may take a while to get used to, but in the long run a sled is your best bet.

Sleds can be designed to carry all the equipment you need to camp in snow. Pulling a sled will be a little difficult at first, somewhat like the first time you took a canoe trip and learned to paddle and portage your canoe. As with the canoe, you will find that sometimes the going will be easy, but going up hills and even steep downgrades will take both energy and practice. Learning how to travel by sled will make your snow outings a real pleasure.

There are several excellent manuals to get you started snowshoeing, backpacking, and skiing. But there are not many places in this country to learn about sled travel, so this manual will give you more on the basics of sled travel.

People in northern climates have used sleds of various types, either pulling them themselves or using draft animals to do the work, since before the time of writing. Many pictographs and petroglyphs show that sleds were in use thousands of years ago. All three of the traditional cultures upon which Okpik is based use sleds of some type. The Okpik program combines these into a sled well adapted for camping in the snow.

The Inuit used sleds made of skins, and even of frozen fish, as well as those made of wood. They either pulled their sleds themselves or used dogs. The sleds of the Inuit formed the models for Arctic and Antarctic explorers. Peary, Scott, Nansen, and Amundsen all used Inuit-style sleds for their expeditions. One recent use of sleds of this type was the Will Steger Expedition to the North Pole in 1986.

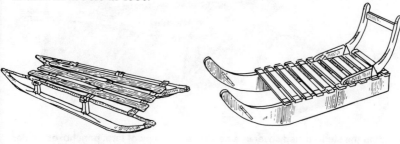

Nansen-style sled   **Inuit-style sled called a Komatik**

North American Indians did not have the windblown, packed snow of the high Arctic, so their sleds took more the form of what we call the toboggan. They later used dogs, and even horses, for pulling sleds, but they usually traveled little during the winter months, and when they did, pulled the sleds themselves.

When the North American fur trade was in full swing, toboggans were used for freighting. They got larger and larger, and were usually pulled by draft animals.

The Laplanders' sleds were pulled by their draft animals, the reindeer. These sleds, similar to small boats, were called *akjas*. Since they are used in deep snow as well as in the high Arctic, akjas represent a combination of the sled styles of the Inuit and American Indian.

Lapland sled called an Akja. It is from this sled that we get the beginnings of the contemporary trail sled called an ahkio.

A modern adaptation of the akja, called the *ahkio,* has been used on many modern expeditions. It can be pulled by campers or by draft animals.

Loading a Sled. When loading a sled, it is important to remember not to overload. The usual weight of equipment for an individual camper is between 60 and 80 pounds. This is a perfect weight for your sled. The equipment will include all materials necessary for you to camp comfortably. It will include your share of the shelter, the cooking equipment, and the food, as well as your personal belongings.

Loading the sled—a sled cover can be almost any type of tarp, poncho, or similar cloth. Skis, snowshoes, or tools can be lashed on the top of the sled.

A common mistake is to stack the equipment on the sled so that the center of gravity is very high. To correctly pack the sled, lay each item the full length of the sled, with the heaviest items on the bottom. Try to have the height of the finished load no more than a foot. A waterproof cover such as a poncho will protect the contents from the weather and keep you from losing items as you travel.

In fastening the cover, lace the load so that there is one area where you can keep items you might need enroute. After the cover is laced, you can put snowshoes or skis on top. A shovel and other items needed for setting up a camp can also be laced to the top. If you are fishing, your auger will, of course, be on top of the sled.

Pulling the Sled. Learning to pull a sled will involve learning a few tricks, and then practicing. After you have mastered the correct techniques, you will find that the sled will be a tremendous help to you. When training for

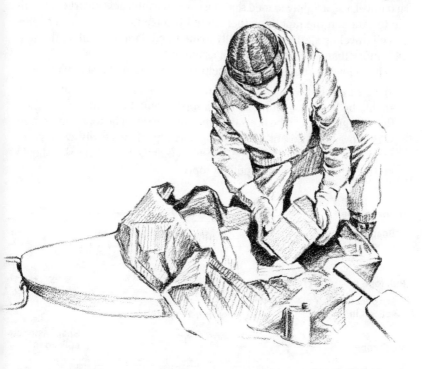

Loading the sled. Heavy items should be packed close to the bottom.

sled travel, use a lightly loaded sled: Just as you would never start out learning to canoe in the rapids, neither should you try to learn the techniques of sled travel by starting with a fully loaded sled. Practice pulling the sled with more than one person as well as alone.

The following suggestions will help you learn to pull a sled with ease:

• Make sure that the pulling device (poles or rope) is long enough. Poles should be at least 5 feet long and a rope should be a little longer than that. A rigid pole can be used any time you use skis. The rope can be used with snowshoes, skis, or when hiking. It is a good idea to always have an extra rope for emergencies. The "mush" rope at the back of the sled should be the same length as the pulling rope.

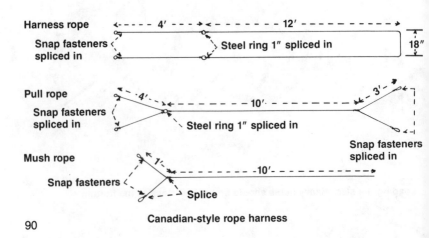

Canadian-style rope harness

Uphill travel is the most difficult.

- The harness that you wear should be attached to a belt. This is so the pull will be from your midsection. It is necessary to have either a strap over your shoulder or a regular shoulder harness so that a waist belt will be held up when you stop, or when the pulling is difficult. If you use a shoulder harness, you can also shift the weight of the pull to your shoulders from time to time. There are many different harness arrangements, each with good points. Choose one that you feel will be best for you.

Different pulling techniques with two people

Even though you will generally pull the sled by yourself, during uphill travel and other difficult times, two or more persons may be needed to pull a sled. When more than one person pulls a sled, it is still best to stay in single file. The towing devices should be long enough to give plenty of room between pullers. At times you may want someone at the rear of the sled. The person at the rear will control the back of the sled, move the sled from side to side, and provide a brake when going down a steep grade.

For sled travel on level and rolling paths (if the snow is not very deep), wear either snowshoes or skis. For rugged uphill travel or steep downgrades, snowshoes are best. After you have become acquainted with your sled and skis, you may want to use skis for more of your sled travel.

Travel Safety

Of course, you need to be conscious of safety when traveling in cold-weather conditions, and always use the buddy system. One danger that you may face is falling through thin ice, or into a hole in the ice. The ice awl, a simple, easily made tool, should be part of every cold-weather camper's equipment.

Use of these "lifesavers" is described in the following article, which appeared in the 1927 BSA handbook *Winter Camping*.

"Another mighty good practice that is widely used abroad as a matter of individual precaution is for each member of the party to carry a pair of 'ice awls.' These are ordinary awls such as you can buy for 5 or 10 cents in any hardware store; cut off the points so that only $5/8$ inch of metal remains protruding from the wooden handle, and file each to a rounded point not necessarily sharp. Drill a hole through the handle, near the top, and fasten a stout piece of cord to each, about the length of your arm.

"The awls should be carried in the breast pocket on the outside of your shirt or mackinaw, with a cord wound around them and fastened to a buttonhole or with a safety pin to the inside of the pocket. The points may be protected by sticking them into corks or into rubber stoppers such as are commonly used on ammonia bottles. A more presentable outfit can be made up with a small case of leather or canvas having a slight piece of metal at the bottom, or a double thickness of material, to protect the points.

"In case of sliding off the edge of ice into open water or going through a large hole, the awls can be quickly withdrawn and, holding them like daggers, can be used as claws to pull yourself out flat on the ice and away from the edge. There is no way your bare hands could get a grip on the smooth ice, and if you attempted to lift yourself out or place your knee on the edge to climb out, your weight would break the edges of the ice and only enlarge the hole and let you in for another ducking. Pull yourself out flat on your stomach and remain that way until you are safely away from the thin ice.

"The next most important precaution is to wear good woolen garments. Equipped in this manner there is no paralyzing breath taking shock when you hit the water, and sliding into a hole is hardly more serious than jumping feet first into the water in the summer. The serious part of ice accidents, like all other so-called accidents, arises from panic and ignorance mainly due to the fact that you have heard over and over again vague tales of going through the ice and not coming up through the same hole again, and you have mentally pictured the shock of jumping into icy waters as being a thousand times more breath-taking than stepping under an unexpectedly cold shower. Under a shower, the water acts directly on your skin; going into the ice, the water requires pretty near a full minute or more to soak through ordinary winter clothing, and if the material is all wool there is no sudden shock of cold, nor do you feel particularly cold after coming out."

Chapter 8

Making Equipment and Clothing

Making camping equipment has always been a specialty of members of the Boy Scouts of America. Many projects, including patterns and descriptions, have been shared through training courses and periodicals. *Boys' Life* reprints are an excellent source of instructions on making your own equipment. Several reprinted articles are in appendix E.

You were introduced to the Okpik clothing system in chapter 3. The items in this chapter can help make your cold-weather camping more enjoyable. Choose the ones that suit your needs and camping area. You will find that some projects can be completed in one evening, while others take several days. Choose the projects that fit your schedule.

Equipment

The "Easiest" Fire Starter

This fire starter takes only a few minutes to make. It doesn't require heating paraffin. It is easy to keep, and it works every time.

Materials

- Cotton
- Petroleum jelly
- 35mm film can

Instructions

1. Take a wad of cotton about the size of a tennis ball and an amount of petroleum jelly about the size of a marble. Mix them together for a few minutes. The cotton should feel covered, but not sticky. If it feels too sticky, add more cotton; if not sticky enough, add petroleum jelly.

2. Pack tightly in a film can or other small container.

3. To use, pull out a small amount and fluff it so that it has plenty of air spaces. If you are using a BSA Hot Spark fire starter, scrape a little of the bar on the cotton, then strike a light. Make sure you have prepared for your fire with tinder, kindling, and fuel wood.

Methods of preparing tinder and fuel for a cold-weather fire

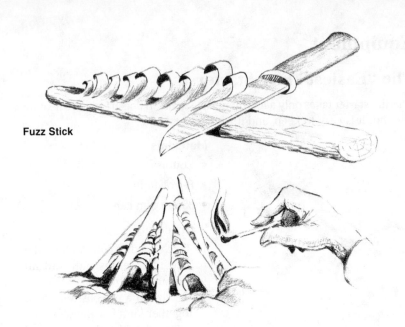

Fuzz Stick

Fuzz sticks used as kindling

Setting up a proper cold-weather fire

Wooden Snow Scoop

These snow scoops are made from plywood. Three styles are illustrated.

Materials

- ¼-inch-thick exterior grade plywood
- Metal for edge, if desired
- Cord for a handle (if design so indicates)

Instructions

1. Cut the scoop from the plywood (we suggest the dimensions in the illustrations).
2. Attach metal to the edge, if desired.
3. Attach a cord handle, if desired.

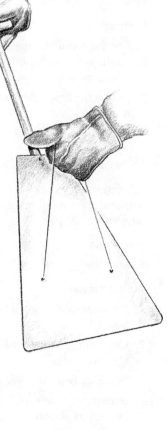

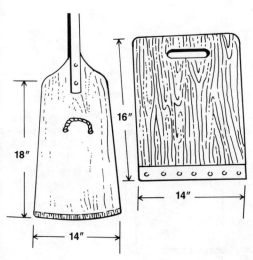

Wooden snow scoop

Ice Awls

You can easily make your own ice awls (called "lifesavers" in the 1927 BSA *Winter Camping* handbook).

Materials

Two pieces of wooden dowel or two pieces of an old broom handle.

Instructions

1. Carefully drill a hole in one end of each piece of wood and insert a 16-penny nail.

2. Cut off the top of the nail and file it to a point.

3. Protect the points with corks.

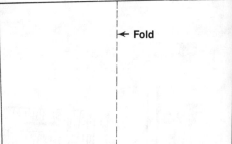

Water Bottle Pouch

You can make a pouch for any size or shape water bottle with little effort.

Materials

Scrap fabric

Instructions

1. Measure your bottle or pouch.

2. Cut fabric and fold as shown.

3. Stitch on two sides.

4. If desired, make squared corners as shown.

5. Turn inside out and attach a neck cord as shown.

6. Add a drawstring in the top, if you like.

←| Fold

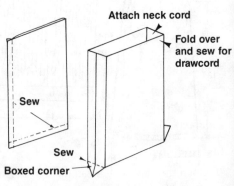

Attach neck cord

Fold over and sew for drawcord

Sew

Sew

Boxed corner

Water Bottle Pouch

Anaotark (Inuit snow beater)

The snow must be beaten from clothing before or immediately after entering a warm shelter so clothing does not get wet, which destroys its insulating properties. The Inuit made their anaotarks from wood, bone, or the antler of the caribou. You can make yours from wood.

Materials

A piece of wood about 1 foot long and about 3 inches wide

Instructions

Shape the wood to match one of the illustrations. The tip should be small so that you can get in small places such as between seams of clothing and footwear.

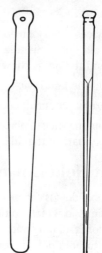

Kodilik (an Inuit stove)

This simple stove is easy to make. It can be used for light or for heating water in small utensils. The kodilik is a good emergency item that can be carried in a small space.

Materials

- Rectangular can such as sardines come in
- Wicking
- Cooking oil
- Small stone

Instructions

1. Open the can using a can opener instead of the key that is usually provided. (Save the lid—you will need it in the next step.)

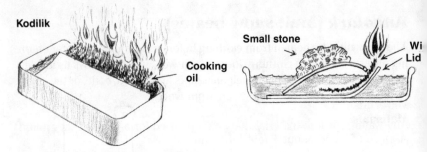

Kodilik

Small stone

Cooking oil

Wi
Lid

2. Bend the lid as shown in the second illustration.

3. Add the lamp wick.

4. Carefully pour in cooking oil. (After use, store the oil in a bottle.)

5. Hold the wick in place with a small stone and another piece of metal (possibly part of the lid).

Tent Hold-Downs and Stove Supports

Tent hold-downs can be used for holding the corners of your tent or for other situations in which you need a secure spot in the snow. They can also be used for insulating and supporting your stove as well as to provide an ideal trivet to hold pots in your snowy kitchen.

Materials

Lightweight ¼-inch plywood scraps, 12 inches square

Instructions

1. Round the corners so they will not puncture anything when packed.

2. Drill a hole in the center.

3. Varnish thickly so snow will not stick, as it will to unprotected materials.

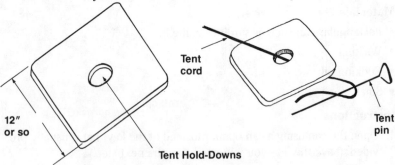

Tent
cord

12"
or so

Tent
pin

Tent Hold-Downs

Windsack *(Vindsekk)*

The windsack is a double tarp with three sides sewn shut. These are very popular in Scandanavian countries. They can be used as a sled cover or a ground cover in your tent, as well as an emergency shelter.

Materials

Any water-repellent material that could be used for a lightweight ground cloth.

Size

The size depends on your needs. A popular size is 7 feet by 8 feet.

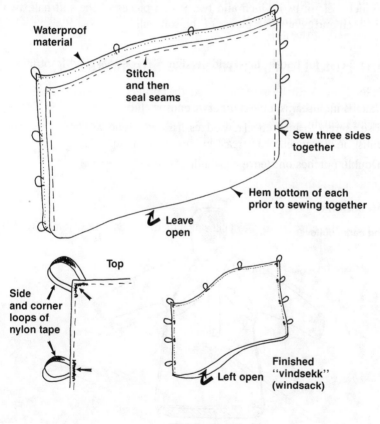

Waterproof material

Stitch and then seal seams

Sew three sides together

Hem bottom of each prior to sewing together

Leave open

Top

Side and corner loops of nylon tape

Finished "vindsekk" (windsack)

Left open

Windsack

Okpik Clothing System

Wind Parka Pullover

A wind parka pullover provides added protection in windy weather.

Materials:

- Main fabric
- A 22-inch nonseparating zipper
- Cord for hood and hem (preferably elastic cord)
- 4 cord pulls
- ⅝-inch Velcro: two 3-inch and two 9-inch pieces of the stiff half; two 5½-inch and two 9-inch pieces of the soft half
- 5 snaps
- Interfacing for pocket flaps and beadings, sleeve tabs, and front flies

Notes

- Take ½-inch seams, unless otherwise instructed.
- Use a serger to finish off all raw edges. If a serger is not available, the edges must be zigzagged or overcast in another manner.
- Double notches on sleeve caps indicate front.

Wind parka pullover

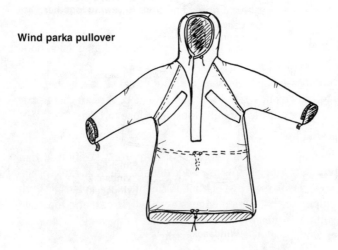

Garment Construction

1. Place soft sides of 9-inch Velcro on right side of pocket flaps, centering on punch holes. Stitch all the way around. Fold flaps in half at notches, right sides together. Add interfacing, and stitch ends using ¼-inch seams. Turn flaps and topstitch finished edges ⅛-inch from edge. Serge unfinished edges together. Fold in half lengthwise with wrong sides facing each other. Serge all three raw sides together.

2. Place stiff sides of 9-inch Velcro on right side of front, centering on punch holes. Stitch in place. Cut a straight slash between pocket punch holes. Place pocket beadings on right side of front, having serged edges even with slash. Extend 1-inch past slash on both ends. Stitch in place, using ⅜-inch seams and extending ½-inch past slash ends. Make V-shaped slashes on each end from punch hole to end of stitching. Turn beadings, flipping ends to wrong side. From inside, stitch ends of beading to V, as close to pocket end as possible. On outside of garment, with seam allowances turned toward body, topstitch close to edge around outside of beading. Tack ends of pocket opening securely. With Velcro side showing, place flaps on right side of front. Serge edges even with topstitching of upper beading. Center flap down over seam allowance, and topstitch ¼-inch from folded edge. Velcro on flap and body should match.

3. Join center seams of both hoods, with right sides facing. Match notches. Join shoulder seams of lining. Join hood lining to lining, with right sides together, matching notches to shoulder seams and stitch pivoting at corners. Serge bottom edge of front lining and back all the way across bottom of hood.

4. Join shoulder seams of body, with right sides together. Join outside hood to body as in lining.

5. Fold both front flies in half at notches, with both right sides together. Add interfacing and stitch ends, using ¼-inch seams. Turn flies and serge raw edges together. On outside fly only, topstitch close to edge.

6. Set zipper as follows:

   • Place zipper, face down, on right side of right front. Position so that zipper teeth start 1 inch below raw edge of hood opening. Edge of zipper tape is even with raw edge of front. Baste into place. Set inside front fly over zipper, so that serged edge is even with front, and top edge with beginning of zipper teeth. Stitch in place using ¼-inch seam and extending ½ inch below bottom of slash.

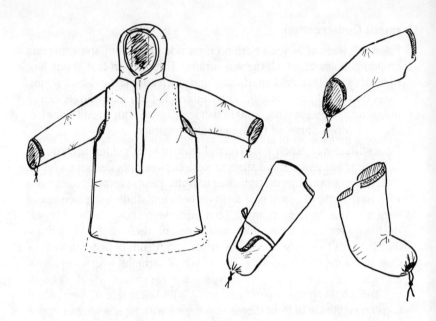

- Open zipper. With right sides together, stitch remaining zipper tape to left side of front, in same manner, omitting fly. Close zipper and stitch bottom of slash from wrong side. Stitch from seam to seam, using ½-inch seam allowance and catching bottom of zipper and inside fly. Can be clipped in V.

- Open zipper. Place lining onto shell, with right sides together. Match hood seams and have edges even. Starting at bottom of zipper, stitch lining to shell using ¼-inch seams. Above zipper teeth on each side, leave a ½-inch opening for cord. Stitch hood opening edge ¼ inch at same time (with zipper sandwiched between lining and shell). Tuck lining to inside. From inside, stitch bottom of zipper opening to lining, using ½-inch seams.

7. From right side, starting at zipper teeth, topstitch, close to edge, all the way around zipper, ending at top of teeth on other side. Topstitch close to edge of hood opening. Place cord in hood so it comes out at openings above zipper. Topstitch hood again, about ½ inch to ¾ inch from previous stitching, tunneling in the cord. Tack cord at center top of hood.

8. Place outside fly on right side of left front. Have serged edges even with zipper topstitching. Bring it up as high as you can without catching cord.

Stitch in place ¼ inch from serged edge. Turn fly over seam allowance and topstitch down ¼ inch from folded edge. Topstitch bottom of outside fly down, close to edge.

9. Serge lining to shell at arm holes. Serge lining to front at side seams. Making sure garment is laying flat, stitch bottom of front lining to body. This forms the pocket bags.

10. Place 3-inch pieces of stiff Velcro on right side of sleeve tabs. Position so they are straight with fold line and about ⅜ inch away from it, and the short end of tab. Stitch in place. Fold in half at notches, right sides together. Add interfacing and stitch (¼ inch from edge) longest and shortest edges together. Turn and topstitch close to edge on all finished sides. Serge raw edges together.

11. Serge bottom edges of sleeves. Place 5½-inch pieces of soft Velcro on right side of sleeves, at punch holes. Stitch in place. Place tabs on sleeves at notches. Have folded edges down and raw edges even. (Velcro pieces should be facing each other). Staystitch in place, close to raw edges.

12. With right sides together, join sleeves to armholes (see notes). Match notch to shoulder seams. Join underarm seams from sleeve end to hem. Hem sleeves at notches.

13. Serge hem edge of garment. Make two small buttonholes at front button, where indicated by punch holes. Pull cord to right side through these holes. Hem garment at notches, tunneling in cord. Tack cord at center back.

14. Place cord pulls (four of them) at each cord end.

15. Evenly space five snaps down outside front fly.

Vest with Detachable Sleeves

Materials

- Main fabric
- 2-inch bias binding for sleeve tops, armholes, and entire outside edge of garment
- 1-inch Velcro (both sides) for sleeve attachment and front closure
- Cord for sleeve ends
- 2 cord pulls
- Lightweight fabric for facings

Notes

- Take ½-inch seams, unless otherwise instructed.

- Use a serger to finish off all raw edges. If a serger is not available, the edges must be zigzagged or overcast in another manner.

- The binding on this garment is sewed as follows: With right side of binding facing wrong side of fabric, and raw edges even, stitch in place with ⅜-inch seam, stretching or easing in where necessary. Turn facing to right side of fabric, over seams. Turn under raw edge ⅜ inch and topstitch close to edge from the right side.

Garment Construction

Vest

1. With right side of right front facing you, lay facing right side up, matching raw edges. Staystitch raw edges together. Turn under ¼ inch on remaining edge, and topstitch close to edge. Place left facing, right side up, on wrong side of left front, and stitch the same.

2. Join shoulder seams with right sides together.

3. Join armhole facings, front to back, at shoulder seams, matching notches. Serge unnotched edges of facings. Set facings, right sides up, on wrong sides of armholes, matching notches and shoulder seams. Topstitch close to edge on all sides.

4. Bind armholes (see notes).

Vest (with or without sleeves)

Hood

Can be made with removable sleeves

5. Cut pieces of 1-inch Velcro shorter than the total length of the armhole facings. Center soft half on facing and stitch all the way around.

6. Lay the collars wrong sides together and staystitch all the way around. Sew the collar facings on ends of collars, same as for fronts (on opposite sides). Serge neck edge of collar and stitch to neck edge with right sides facing. Match front facings and notches.

7. Bind garment all the way around collar, down fronts, and hem.

8. Cut five 2-inch lengths of 1-inch Velcro. Starting at the center of the collar, evenly space them horizontally, down the center of front facings. Use stiff half on right front.

Sleeves

1. Join underarm seam and around thumb with right sides together. To join sleeve seams, match notches and stitch from top about ½ inch from edge leaving a ½-inch opening.

2. Bind top of sleeve (see notes, above).

3. Serge bottom edges of sleeves. Hem at notches, tunneling in cord. Bring cord out through opening.

4. Place cord pulls.

5. Set other half of armhole Velcro (stiff half) on right side of sleeve cap, and center between shapings. Stitch all the way around.

Wind Pants

Materials

- Main fabric
- Cord (preferably elastic) for waist, leg openings, and suspender loops
- 9-inch pant zipper
- 4 cord pulls
- 1 snap
- Six pieces of 1-inch by 2-inch Velcro (both sides) for front pocket flaps
- Two pieces 1-inch by 1½-inch Velcro (both sides) for back pocket
- Interfacing for pocket flaps, back pocket edge, and undersnaps

Notes

- Take ½-inch seams, unless otherwise instructed.
- Use a serger to finish off all raw edges. If a serger is not available, the edges must be zigzagged or overcast in another manner.
- You may also use ½-inch elastic, cut to fit, for the legs and waist of pant, if you tack down the ends. This will eliminate the cord, buttonholes, and the cord pulls. You will still need a small amount of cord for the suspender loops, if they are desired.

Garment Construction

1. If using cord, make small buttonholes at bottom of front legs and each front waist, where indicated by punch holes.
2. Serge waist and hem edges of fronts and backs. Also serge front fly, crotch seam, and pocket opening (between notches), on both sides. Clip seam allowance at notches.
3. Fold zipper fly at notches with wrong sides together, and serge all three raw edges.
4. With right sides together, join front crotch seam to 1 inch above notch at bottom of right front fly.
5. Set zipper as follows:
   - With right sides facing, place zipper on right front, with top of zipper at zipper notch and zipper tape ½ inch from raw edge of fly. Stitch down center of zipper tape. Turn and topstitch close to edge, all the way from waist to bottom of zipper.
   - Turn zipper to original position, and place zipper fly on right side with right edges of top and fly even. Using ¼-inch seam, stitch in place all the way from waist to bottom.
   - On left front, fold fly at notch to wrong side evenly. With wrong side of front facing, place right side of remaining zipper edge over fly, positioning so top of zipper is even with zipper notch and zipper teeth are in center of fly. Starting at waist edge, stitch, catching edge of zipper tape and continuing in the shape of the fly, all the way to crotch seam.
   - Tack zipper fly to left front fly edge for about 1 inch at bottom side.
6. Set soft half of ⅝-inch Velcro to right side of front pocket flaps, positioning at punch holes. Stitch all the way around. Fold pocket flaps in half at notches, having right side of fabric together. Place interfacing on top

and stitch both ends at ¼ inch. Turn flaps and topstitch finished edges ¼ inch from edge. Serge raw edges together.

7. Turn pants ½ inch to wrong side between notches, and topstitch ⅜ inch from folded edge. Place stiff half of ⅝-inch Velcro on right side of fronts, positioning at punch holes. Stitch all the way around.

8. Serge top of back pocket with interfacing. Turn at notches and hem. Place 2 pieces of 1-inch Velcro (hard halves), on right side of pocket at punch holes. Stitch all the way around. Turn raw edges of pocket under ½ inch, and position pocket on right side of the right back, at punch holes, extending ⅜ inch above and beyond marks. Topstitch pocket to pant ⅛ inch from edge, tacking well at tops. Topstitch again, ¼ inch from previous stitching. Place soft halves of 1-inch Velcro on right side of back pocket flaps, positioning on punch holes. Stitch all the way around. Fold pocket flaps at notches, right sides together, at notches, adding interfacing. Stitch ends using ¼-inch seam. Turn flaps and topstitch ⅛ inch from edge on finished sides. Stitch again ¼ inch from previous stitching. Serge raw edges together. With Velcro side of flap showing and serged edge down, position serged edge evenly at punch holes, extending ⅜ inch on both sides. Stitch to back, ¼ inch from serged edge. Turn flap down and topstitch in place, ¼ inch from top edge. Velcro should match up when pocket is closed.

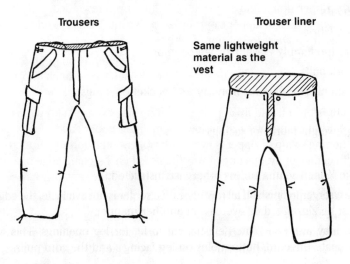

Trousers

Trouser liner

Same lightweight material as the vest

9. With right sides together, stitch the back crotch seam. Stitch backs to fronts at side seams, stitching back front pocket flaps to back between notches. Do not catch front between pocket notches. Tack pocket flaps securely towards front at top and bottom, extending ½ inch on each side of side seam. With right sides together, join fronts to backs at inseams.

10. Hem leg openings at notches, tunneling cord so it is on the outside between buttonholes, and tack the ends at center back.

11. Melt raw edge of nylon webbing so it won't ravel.

12. Place cord in waist so it comes out at buttonholes. Place small squares of interfacing at tops of zipper where the snaps will be. Fold over at hemline notches. Stitch waist down, tunneling cord and placing button tabs at notches and side seams. Tack cord at center back.

13. Tack another piece of cording on inside of each front, from front button tab to side seam button tab. (These loops are for suspenders.)

14. Place one snap above zipper at waist.

15. Sew buttons on tabs inside pants.

16. Place cord pulls (one on each leg, and one on each front waist).

Wind Pants Liner

Materials
- Main fabric
- Cord (preferably elastic) for leg openings
- 2 cord pulls
- 2-inch bias binding for front fly and pocket openings
- 1 button
- Lightweight fabric for facings

Notes
- Take ½-inch seams, unless otherwise instructed.
- Use a serger to finish off all raw edges. If a serger is not available, the edges must be zigzagged or overcast in another manner.
- You may also use ½-inch elastic, cut to fit, for leg openings. This will eliminate the cord, buttonholes on leg facings, and the cord pulls.

- The binding on this garment is sewed as follows: With right side of binding facing wrong side of fabric, and raw edges even, stitch in place with ⅜-inch seam, stretching or easing in where necessary. Turn facing to right side of fabric, over seams. Turn under raw edge ⅜ inch and topstitch close to edge from the right side.

Garment Construction

1. Serge all long, unnotched edges of facings (3 waist and 2 leg).

2. With rights side facing, join the fronts at short crotch seam. Join backs at crotch seam. With right sides together, join the fronts to the backs at the side seams, to pocket openings. Join inseams.

3. Bind front fly openings and both pocket openings.

4. With right sides together, join waist facings to pant, matching notches. Turn facings to wrong side of pant and topstitch close to edge all the way around, turning ends under as necessary.

5. Make buttonholes at waist, where indicated by punch holes. Make all buttonholes vertical, except the one at the front which should be made horizontal.

6. If using cord, make two buttonholes, about 1 inch apart, at center of front by facings.

7. With right sides together, join ends of the leg facings with cord or elastic ends attached. If using cord, leave it out between buttonholes. Stitch facings to leg openings, with right sides together, matching notches and

Wind pant   **Wind pant liner**

Windproof material or waterproof in wet cold areas

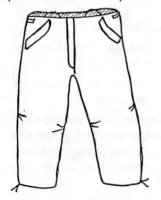
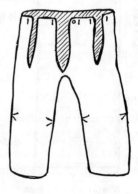

seams. Turn facings to wrong side and stitch down close to edge, tunneling the cord or elastic inside. Tack cord at center back.

8. Place cord pulls.
9. Sew buttons to front.

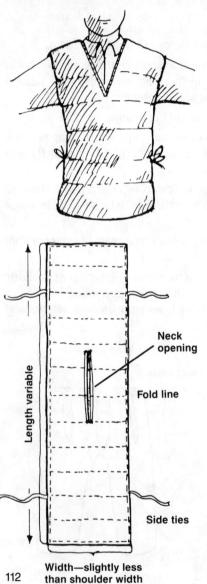

Neck opening

Fold line

Length variable

Side ties

Width—slightly less than shoulder width

Other Clothing

Vest

This simple vest comes from the Boy Scouts of Sweden. It can be made in one evening and will work well for any type of cold-weather outing.

Materials

- Old blanket, insulating material, or 1-inch foam materials as described in the *Fieldbook*
- Two or four pieces of cord for ties

Instructions

1. Cut the vest to fit the wearer.
2. Use one or two sets of ties on the sides.
3. Make a slit for the neck opening. The opening can be finished off with edging or even a collar, if desired.

Wristlets

Before you throw away that worn pair of socks, you may want to try making one of the wristlets shown. In Europe, these are called pulse warmers. They can be worn by themselves in mild weather, or with gloves or mittens in colder weather. They also work great in the sleeping bag. Wristlets work because they protect your wrist area. The blood carrying the warmth to your fingers is better protected this way.

Materials

Worn pair of socks

Instructions

1. Cut off the top of a pair of worn-out socks.
2. Sew together as shown in one of the illustrations and you will have a great pair of wristlets.

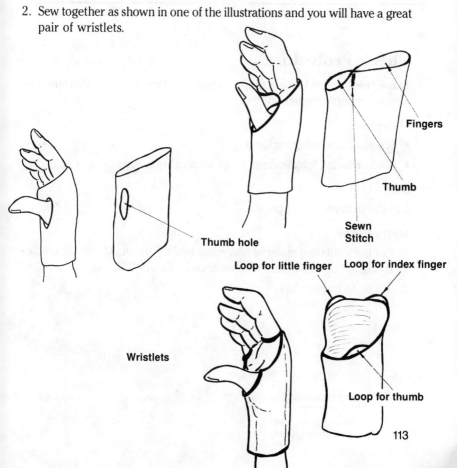

Fingers

Thumb

Sewn Stitch

Thumb hole

Loop for little finger   Loop for index finger

Wristlets

Loop for thumb

113

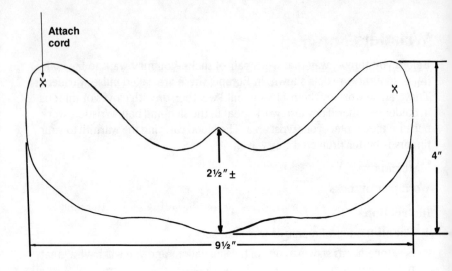

Attach
cord

X   X

2½" ±

4"

9½"

Cheek Protectors

These cheek protectors are simple to make and are really good in any cold-weather camping situation.

Materials
- Scraps of insulating material
- Cord or lacing long enough to go around your head

Size
Use the pattern on this page.

Instructions
1. Cut the insulating material according to the pattern. Attach the cord or lacing to the two outer curves marked with an "X."
2. Adjust to fit your face.

Swedish Footwraps

Swedish footwraps can be used with or without socks. They keep your feet warm and are easy to dry. They should be worn inside boots, mukluks, moccasins, etc.

Materials

- Insulating material
- Cord long enough to tie around the ankle

Size

For adults, 20″ × 20″—vary the size according to the size of the foot.

Instructions

Cut two footwraps and fold over the foot, as shown. Tie at the ankle.

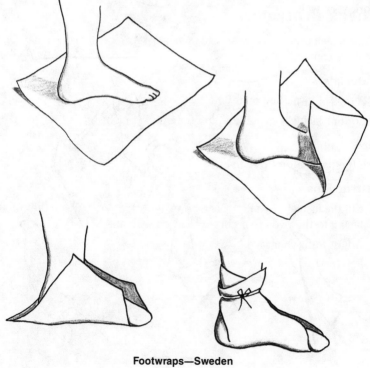

Footwraps—Sweden

Finnish Footwraps

These are similar to the Swedish models, but different enough to be interesting. Finnish footwraps are cut in a rectangle instead of a square. They do not need a cord to time them since they are made to tuck into the top.

Materials

Insulating material

Size

For adults: 21″ × 26″—vary the rectangle proportionally to the size of the foot.

Instructions

Wrap as shown in the illustration. It will take a little practice, but they work very well.

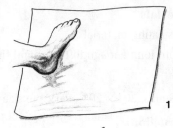

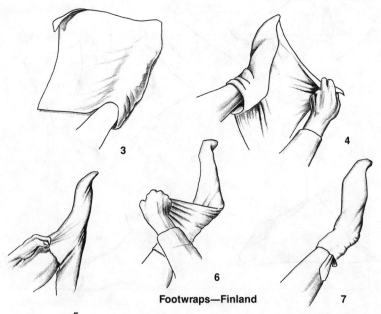

Footwraps—Finland

116

Fotposer

The *fotposer* (Norwegian) is a waterproof covering for your feet and lower legs. It is very useful when building snow shelters. These foot and leg protectors are worn directly over your boots and should come up above your ankle at the top.

Materials

- Waterproof fabric such as that used for rain jackets
- Nylon cord for ties

Size

The size is determined by your boot size and the length of your leg.

Instructions

1. Cut as illustrated.
2. Sew on extra support piece, turning under raw edge as shown.
3. Fold each fotposer in half lengthwise and sew around edges, as shown.

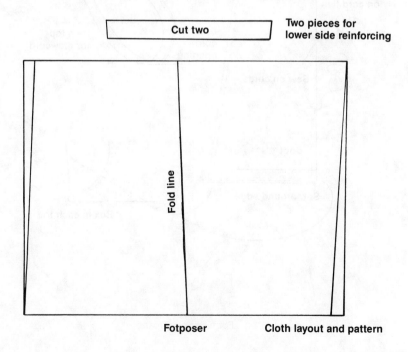

117

Fotposer

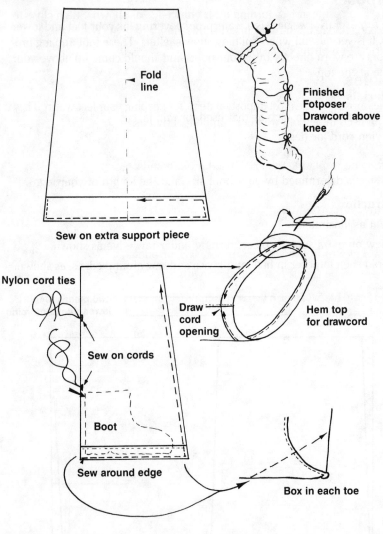

Fold line

Sew on extra support piece

Finished Fotposer Drawcord above knee

Nylon cord ties

Draw cord opening

Hem top for drawcord

Sew on cords

Boot

Sew around edge

Box in each toe

4. Turn right side out and sew on cords for ties.

5. Turn in casing at top, turning under raw edge as shown. Stitch close to edge, leaving opening to insert drawstring.

6. Insert drawstring in casing.

Insoles

Insoles are one of the most important items for keeping your feet warm. They can be used in all cold-weather camping activities.

Materials

Scrap foam insulating material, used ground pads, etc.

Size

Use the patterns on this page for your insoles.

Instructions

1. Cut foam to fit inside shoes, moccasins, or boots.

2. Place inside shoes, moccasins, or boots.

Note: Scrap foam can also be used to make sitting pads and insulating items for the cold-weather kitchen.

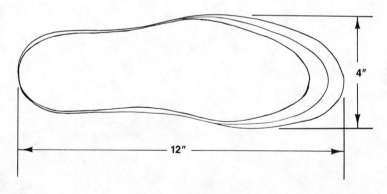

Insoles
(Check size or length of foot.)

"Why Go Winter Camping?" is reproduced for historical purposes as appendix A from BSA's *Winter Camping* manual, published in 1927. Read through this information to see the similarities and differences in the way things were then and the way they are now.

Appendix A

Why Go Winter Camping?

The Boy Scouts of America have blazed the trail of camping and other outdoor activities for boys. Winter camps and all-weather hikes are a comparatively new phase of Scouting, but they have grown so rapidly in interest that some communities report more boys in short term and winter camps during the school year than in all the outdoor activities of the summer vacation period.

Organized winter camping has been so new that only meager information could be found in print on the subject, although its popularity had created a great demand from leaders for advice and program material. The efforts of our Camping and Editorial Departments have made it possible now, to present a wealth of material from Council Officers, Scoutmasters, explorers and winter sports experts which has stood the test of actual experience.

While this volume is prepared primarily as a guide for Scoutmasters, it contains material which will be of service to leaders of boys in other organizations.

This limited edition is being published in order that those in whose hands this volume is placed may give us the benefit of their constructive criticism and submit additional material which might be included in later and more complete editions.

It gives me great pleasure to express on behalf of the Boy Scouts of America, our sincere appreciation to those who furnished material and helped in the preparation of this volume for publishing. I commend it enthusiastically to all Scoutmasters who are so devotedly striving to bring to members of their Troops, vigorous, outdoor activities toward the development of character and good citizenship.

James E. West, Chief Scout Executive

Exerpt from *Winter Camping.* New York: Boy Scouts of America, 1927.

Why Camp in Winter?

"A Scout walks through the woods with silent tread. His eyes are keen and he sees many things that others do not see. He sees tracks and signs which reveal to him the nature and habits of the creatures that made them. He knows how to stalk birds and animals and study them in their natural haunts."

Do you remember how you thrilled when you first read those words in the Handbook for Boys? That is what boys come into Scouting to get—Scoutcraft, inspiration, education, not just a week or two at the Council Camp in the summer, but all year around! It can be done, Mr. Scoutmaster. Others, no better qualified than you, have gone ahead and developed a hiking and camping Troop.

Put yourself in the place of the Scout for the moment—when, full of enthusiasm, imagination, and wonderful ideas, he joined the Troop. He joined expecting to find Scouting what he had dreamed it to be, an adventure in the out-of-doors—and woke up in the Troop to find the command of "patrols right, and patrols left" in addition to classes, lectures and talks.

It is the out-door Troop that does real Scouting, the Scouting of character building and citizenship training, as well as the Scouting of cooking, trailing, and taking care of one's self in the open. The boys learn self-reliance and dependability; the ways of the woods and its creatures. The Scoutmaster gets a new grip on his Troop, developing cooperation and loyalty.

Many Troops are camping Troops—in Spring, Summer, and Fall (late Spring and very early Fall). But in Winter—"Ah, there's the rub!"

The Boy Scouts of America stand for a YEAR-AROUND hiking and camping program. Are you with us?

Under All Conditions

No Scoutmaster can be satisfied that the Scouts have really met the requirements, are actually living up to the Scout Motto, unless they are *prepared* to meet them under *all* conditions.

It may not be in a city street that the Scout must suddenly depend upon his first aid knowledge to save a human life, but in the midst of a howling blizzard, 40 miles from the doctor. The Scout who wins the fire-building contest with carefully prepared fire-board and tinder, may be called upon to use his skill for the comfort of an entire party in the wilderness, during a January thaw. Because of the confidence they feel in Scout training, not only do people place responsibility upon Scouts in an emergency, but Scouts them-

selves, feeling certain of their qualifications, voluntarily assume such responsibility. This confidence can only be justified if the Scout has passed his tests
under conditions that are a real challenge to his ability.

Two Major Problems

There are many advantages that the winter camp has over the summer
camp. Yet many a Troop does parlor Scouting all winter without even a winter hike. They fail to try it, in general, because of two reasons that loom up
to them as problems of magnitude. "There is no cabin, nor even an old barn
that is at all accessible for the Troop—how are we going to keep warm without shelter?"

Such Scoutmasters greatly overestimate the difficulties of winter camping. It is a program, it is true, only for hardy Scouts, for Scouts who are experienced campers, unless they can go to an organized Council camp, or
adequate shelter is available. But hundreds of Scouts camp every year in
tents, when the temperature ranges from 30 degrees above zero to several
degrees below, and enjoy the experience. Some hardy Scouts even sleep in
the open, using ponchos and blankets or sleeping bags. So, the matter of
shelter is not an insurmountable difficulty. The older boys of the Troop can
camp comfortably in tents and will be all the better for the experience. And
the Troop can build a cabin for a permanent camp. Or it may be that on Saturday hikes, some shelter can be discovered—an old barn or an abandoned
shack that can be made weather-proof. And think of the joy, of the challenge,
of meeting the wilderness in its grimmest mood, and conquering it! The zest
of achievement, the bounding energy that thrills you!

What If There Is No Snow?

This brings up the second objection advanced by a large section of the country. "It is all very well for people in the north to talk about winter camp. Skiing and skating, toboganing and ice sports make a carnival out of any camp.
But in this section we don't get enough snow to fill a tea cup. Frozen, bare
ground, or mud—that's our winter camp. What chance for a program?" The
answer to that is "All the chance in the world!" Carry on all the Scout program that you would in a summer camp, with the challenge of winter
weather and the novelty of winter conditions. Practically all the Scout Tests,
except Swimming, should, even in winter, be passed out of doors. There is
in addition a wide variety of activities that are too good to miss because of
a lack of leadership or initiative to organize a winter camp. Study the list

of activities and projects appearing on pages 159 and 163. Winter is an ideal time to go into the open to get away from steam radiators, stuffy rooms and parlor Scouting, and enjoy a real program. Don't den up all winter like a bear because the weather is cold. Get out and enjoy it! You'll come back tingling with life, all set to go again. Scouts don't grow strong and husky indoors, but they do out of doors, and hard as nails. Open air, vigorous physical exercise, wholesome food and regular sleep are a sure cure for indoor stuffiness.

Health Conditions in Winter Especially Advantageous

Many problems of sanitation disappear at the end of the warm weather. The question of refrigeration is answered without the aid of any human agency. Nature may furnish all materials for preserving food free of charge. Flies, mosquitoes and other insect pests are gone and, consequently, demand no special attention from campers. Hurrah! Snakes, lizards, spiders, centipedes and tarantulas no longer urge their company upon you. The dust which, laden with a choice assortment of germs, arose eagerly to meet you in summer, now lies prostrate, conquered by the heavier rainfall, the snow, and the decrease in evaporation of moisture which winter brings to our relief.

No one has any excuse or reason for remaining inactive. Heat, humidity, fear of sunstroke may serve as excuse for laziness in summer. Sometimes these may cause genuine lack of energy. In winter the temperature is such as to encourage and even necessitate vigorous action.

The swimming pool which is the immediate attraction for water sports in summer is still available for boating and sailing in open weather or for ice-boating, skating, hockey, etc., in winter. On the other hand, a swimming pool is not necessary for a winter camp site.

More Vacation Time

Under normal conditions in summer, boys spend most of their time in the open and flourish. In winter school demands most of the day and leaves but little time for outdoor recreation. This is especially true in the cities where a place for winter sports may be lacking. If the boy is at work, in shop, factory, or office, his surroundings are less likely to conform with the standards of physical well-being and his hours for exercise in the open even more limited.

Winter, as the season of many short vacations, is particularly generous in giving opportunities for camping and hiking. Unlikely as this sounds, investigation will prove it true. The usual vacations at Christmas and Easter, the week-ends, Thanksgiving, Columbus Day, Washington's Birthday, Lincoln's Birthday and other special single-day holidays, aggregate between 90 to 100 full days between the of September and the twenty-fifth of June. Nor are these holidays likely to be devoted to activities which leave no time for Scouting. Employment by the single day or single week is not economical from the standpoint of the employer nor very often sought by the schoolboy.

Quite different are the conditions in summer. The entire ten weeks of summer vacation give no more than seventy days in all to be spent in camping, in comparison to over 90 during the school year. In the country, farm work and gardening claim the boy of Scout age. In the city, many boys find it profitable to take a job for the summer months. If the boy is not working, still other conditions may prove an obstacle to his enjoying any camping experience. He may be with his family at a summer home so far from the camp site that his parents are reluctant to let him go to it. It is always true that a large percentage of each community group is prevented from going into a summer camp by circumstances which in winter might not exist at all or only in a very small degree.

Makes Available the Choicest Sites and Equipment

In summer, camping is a diversion for the multitude. Swarms of picnickers and tourists terming themselves campers, infest the desirable sites on the banks of every lake and stream and in the forest clearings. The result is that Scouts in summer must go far afield, often building all their own equipment, in order to find suitable sites where they will not be annoyed by a neighboring horde of pseudo campers. Winter camping is beyond the ability of the novice. The choice sites, splendidly equipped, are then at the disposal of Scouts. The possibility of sites nearer home brings camping within the range of many boys for whom the summer camp is a dream which cannot materialize. The cost of transportation to the summer camp site is often prohibitive for boys of moderate means. General expenses are also reduced by the lower cost of shipping supplies and equipment.

The reduction of distance means that leaders and Scouts will be able to devote to their program of training and recreation those precious hours which might otherwise be spent in railway or steamship travel. And in the limited duration of each winter camp every hour and half hour gained is a vital matter.

Charm of Winter Sports

The charm of winter sports is undeniable. When properly directed they open new avenues through which to appeal to boys and school them in vigorous action. Varied in themselves, these games afford a distinct contrast to the sports and Scout games of summer that may often stimulate waning interest. Most of these are group activities, or may be adapted to give opportunity for team work. All involve constant action—a requirement of the weather itself—and lend themselves readily, when directed in a purposeful fashion, to physical development and the building of a good group spirit.

A Training Period First

No Scoutmaster, however, can take a Troop of boys who are used to overheated rooms, boys whose outdoor exercise consists of a walk to school, out to a winter camp, to sleep in a tent. Football players, after the season's training can stand up under knocks that would have laid them flat in the previous summer. The Troop must be seasoned in the same way. It is not hard to get Scouts enthusiastic over the idea.

Each Scout can start his training by sleeping with wide open windows and taking a daily cold bath.

If the Troop is a hiking Troop, you already know something of the physical endurance of each boy. Hold regular Saturday hikes for a month or six weeks, gradually increasing the distance. Through the week the boys hike by patrols or in smaller units. These hikes must be at a brisk pace, and must be taken under any sort of weather conditions, as no one knows what kind of weather the Troop may encounter in camp. Each boy will thus gain daily in strength, vigor and endurance. Encourage them to experiment in the matter of footgear, clothing, etc., till they discover their individual preferences.

After a few weeks of training, instead of returning from the hike before dinner, hold a council fire in the evening, and hike back in the frosty darkness. If the Scouts are warm and cheerful, husky and happy and unfatigued, you may begin to consider an overnight camp.

One-Day Camps

1—Travel Light

On a one-day camp it is possible as well as desirable, to travel light. No great amount of equipment is necessary. Food supplies and, perhaps, some cooking utensils only need be carried, and these when distributed among the party are no burden at all. The object of the expedition may be such as to require special implements, but as a usual thing, heavy packs and trek carts are so little needed that any Troop which uses them is open to the charge of doing it to give an impression of hardiness.

2—Cook Over Campfires

The only stove needed is a camp-fire. This gives the Scouts the opportunity to prove their abilities as real camp cooks. More credit will therefore, be given to these Scouts who can prepare a palatable dish without any utensils besides those to be found in the woods. In some cases, where the services to be rendered require steady work on the part of the entire group, it may be preferable to take most of the food in ready-to-eat form and cook only the beverage and perhaps one other item on the menu. Under average conditions, it gives better training if all the food is prepared over the camp-fire.

Long Hikes and Gypsy Trips

These trips are designed to train boys in proper methods of transportation, observation and selection of pack and provisions that make it possible to shift camp quickly. First of all, let us emphasize that on hikes means of transportation must be determined in advance. If Scouts are to walk the entire distance, it is the quitter who "hooks a ride" on some passing wagon or automobile, or who leaves the crowd to cut across green fields on some other route than the one over which the Troop must go. The danger of assuming the role of youthful hoboes by "bumming their way" should be avoided. If a share of the distance is to be covered by lifts, hooks, catches or free passes of any sort, these should be arranged for in advance, not begged along the way.

A long hike or gypsy trip needs careful planning and a definite object. The objective may be some place of historical interest or a specially good camp site. Or the trip may be designed to give practice in some phase of Scoutcraft or definite activity, rather than to reach any one particular spot. In any case, certain precautions are necessary. You should get all the information possible as to good stopping places, and sources for buying provisions en route. No Scout should be allowed to go unless he is physically fit. The average of the weakest member of the party is the proper gauge for speed. Forced marches to break records are not only unwise but dangerous. Care of the feet must be considered. The weight of equipment and convenience of packs must be planned so that there will be comfort on the way as well as in camp.

Great care must be exercised to prevent the drinking of impure water. Above all, if Scouts are to make the right impression, they must scrupulously observe all road rules, avoid any catch penny schemes for making money or any appearance of "living off the country" or begging, instead of paying their own way.

Preparations

Leadership

In no other camp is the type of leadership as important as in the winter camp. This subject is discussed in detail in the Section on Business Management. It is vital, because of the serious responsibility that rests upon him, that the leader be a man of strong character and that he be an experienced camper.

Equipment

Equipment for winter is more expensive than for the summer camp. Do not attempt to camp with a scratch outfit. See that Scouts are adequately clothed, and that blankets and other equipment are of the right quality and weight. The period of training will give an opportunity to get together with the necessary articles. No camp should be attempted until the equipment is ready.

Physician's Certificate

A physician's certificate as to his physical ability must be presented by each Scout before he even begins his period of preliminary training. Before the Troop starts for camp, each Scout should have a thorough physical inspection. Even a mild case of sniffles should not be ignored. Pneumonia or other ailments may result. (See also Section on Health, Safety, and Sanitation).

Balanced Program

A carefully planned program is essential. In the summer camp, a certain amount of free time is desirable. But in the winter, unless Scouts are vigorously active, they get cold. There must be no intervals of standing around and waiting for something to happen. Things must move with snap and precision from the moment the Troop unloads its packs until the last ember of the fire is extinguished before they leave for home. A series of suggested programs is presented on page 184, which the Scoutmaster can adapt to his own needs. Opportunity must be given for Scout advancement, and plenty of games of vigorous action. Hikes throughout the neighboring country should be scheduled, and camp Good Turns. If Scouts must fill their own woodpile, details must be assigned. Assign details for dishwashing, cooking and other tasks, also. Plan activities that keep the Troop together. It is hazardous to have small groups scatter too far apart in winter. The tendency of the Scouts to keep together and not far from the fire will help this.

Evening Camp-Fire

The evening program in particular requires careful planning. Evening begins as early as 4:30 to 5 o'clock at some seasons of the year. It is often impossible to sit out of doors around the council fire, and stunts and dramatics that require much room cannot be used in the narrow space of the cabin. The indoor projects of the Troop must be provided as carefully as the outdoor program. The wise leader does not rely on songs and stories and stunts only. A list of suggested handicraft projects adapted to indoor camp is given on page 246, and every Troop will develop others for itself. (See Section on Entertainment.)

Mud

Some leaders of winter camps have declared that the great problem in their camps was mud. Scouts track all out of doors onto the cabin floor, that heavy, sticky mud to which some sections of the country are often reduced between January and March. Old newspapers spread down help this condition. Wearing moccasins in the house is a preventative. A scrubbing brush detail will probably induce all the boys to exercise care and forethought.

Appendix B

BSA Policy on Use of Chemical Fuels (Liquid, Gaseous, or Jellied) December 1989

Purpose

To share the policy and guidelines on the use of chemical fuels by the membership of the Boy Scouts of America.

Background

There are three factors that influence the establishment of Scouting's policy on the use of fuel other than natural wood: (1) The basic purposes of Scouting and its camping program. (2) The protection from hazards of chemical fuels. (3) The necessity of safely adapting to local conditions and practices.

First, it is essential to Scouting's purpose that a boy learn and practice the skills of primitive living. He develops a personal confidence, initiative, and preparation for life as he advances through the Scouting program.

In building a fire he needs to learn the care and use of tools; know about tinder, types of fuel, and how to prepare it. The correct principles of building a fire to cook his food and warm his body, containing fire, and putting it out are essential for his training in campcraft, self-reliance, and preparedness.

The need for adapting to special circumstances, such as lack of natural wood for fuel or the regulations of specific areas where open fires are prohibited for safety or environmental reasons, makes it necessary for Scouts and Scout leaders to learn the skills and safety procedures in using chemical fuel stoves.

Convenience is one of the joys of modern life, but with it goes the necessity of precaution against many hazards.

When any chemical fuel is used for cooking and lighting, it is the fuel which is dangerous—not the stove and lanterns.

Policy and Guidelines

For safety reasons, knowledgeable adult supervision must be provided when Scouts are involved in the storage of chemical fuels, the handling of chemical fuels in the filling of stoves or lanterns, or the lighting of chemical fuels.

Battery-operated lanterns and flashlights should be used by Scouts in camping activities, particularly in and around canvas tentage. No chemical-fueled lantern or stove is to be used inside a tent.

Kerosene, gasoline, or liquefied petroleum fuel lanterns may, when necessary, be used inside permanent buildings or for outdoor lighting. When used indoors there should be adequate ventilation. Strict adherence to the safety standards and instructions of the manufacturers in fueling and lighting such stoves and lanterns must be carried out under the supervision of a responsible and knowledgeable adult.

Both gasoline and kerosene shall be kept in well-marked approved containers (never in a glass container) and stored in a ventilated locked box at a safe distance (minimum 20 feet) from buildings and tents.

Empty liquid petroleum cylinders for portable stoves and lanterns should be returned home or to base camp. They may explode when heated and therefore must never be put in fireplaces or with burnable trash.

The use of liquid fuels for starting any type of fire is prohibited. This includes damp wood, charcoal, and ceremonial camp fires. Solid-type starters are just as effective, are easier to store and carry, and are much safer to use for this purpose.

All types of space heaters that use chemical fuels consume oxygen and must only be used in well-ventilated areas. When used in cabins, camper-trucks, and recreational vehicles, there is not only a fire danger but also lives can be lost from asphyxiation if not well ventilated. Use of charcoal burners indoors can be lethal in causing carbon monoxide poisoning.

Guidelines for Safely Using Chemical Stoves and Lanterns

1. Use compressed or liquid-gas stoves and/or lanterns only with knowledgeable adult supervision, and in Scout facilities only where and when permitted.

2. Operate and maintain regularly according to manufacturer's instructions included with the stove or lantern.

3. Store fuel in approved containers and in storage under adult supervision. Keep all chemical fuel containers away from hot stoves and campfires, and store below 100°F.

4. Let hot stoves and lanterns cool before changing cylinders of compressed gases or refilling from bottles of liquid gas.

5. Refill liquid gas stoves and lanterns a safe distance from any flames, including other stoves, campfires, and personal smoking substances. A commercial camp stove fuel should be used for safety and performance. Pour through a filter funnel. Recap both the device and the fuel container before igniting.

6. Never fuel a stove or lantern inside a cabin; always do this out-of-doors. Do not operate a stove or lantern in an unventilated structure. Provide at least two ventilation openings, one high and one low, to provide oxygen and exhaust for lethal gases. Never fuel, ignite, or operate a stove or lantern in a tent.

7. Place the stove on a level, secure surface before operating. On snow, place insulated support under the stove to prevent melting and tipping.

8. Periodically check fittings on compressed-gas stoves and on pressurized liquid-gas stoves for leakage with soap solution before lighting.

9. When lighting a stove keep fuel bottles and extra canisters well away. Do not hover over the stove when lighting it. Keep your head and body to one side. Open the stove valve quickly for two full turns and light carefully, with head, fingers, and hands to the side of the burner. Then adjust down.

10. Do not leave a lighted stove or lantern unattended.

11. Do not overload the stovetop with extra-heavy pots or large frying pans. If pots over 2 quarts are necessary, set up a separate grill with legs to hold the pot and place stove under grill.

12. Bring empty fuel containers home for disposal. Do not place in or near fires. Empty fuel containers will explode if heated.

Bulk Storage Practices

Camp officials must be especially alert to the tendency to violate these principles by Scout leaders coming into camp with their units. Storage of bulk supplies of any chemical fuels (especially volatile fuels) is a camp maintenance function. Storage and issue of such fuel must be controlled by a responsible adult and be kept under lock and key in Scout camps. Quantities of gasoline in long-term camps must be stored in a properly installed underground tank with pump, and/or must be in compliance with local safety standards and regulations.

Filling tanks for motor vehicles, outboard and inboard motors, and gasoline-powered saws and motors shall always be handled by someone qualified by age and training for this responsibility. All motors are turned off during filling. Enclosed bilges on boats equipped with inboard motors in enclosed spaces must be ventilated by blower for not less than 4 minutes (federal law) to remove fumes before engines are started. All hatches and ports should be closed during fueling and the boat reventilated when fueling is completed. No smoking or open flames are permitted while filling any fuel tanks.

Liquid petroleum storage tanks at permanent camps should be installed by experienced technicians and changed only by the gas distributors. These installations must conform to local regulations. Fuel containers should be surrounded by a chain link fence in a cleared area.

Action

Local councils, through roundtables and volunteer training courses, should make every effort to train unit leaders and assistants in the proper techniques and procedures necessary to safely operate chemically fueled stoves and lanterns. These leaders, in turn, train and supervise youth members in these same skills and procedures.

Appendix C

Personal Protection Items for Cold-Weather Camping

The items listed below are recommended for personal protection in cold weather. They can be carried in either of two ways—both of which are good.

1. Scatter the items throughout your clothing. The advantages include having only a small bulk and weight in any one location; the loss of one item doesn't mean the loss of all; and you will not be as tempted to rob your "emergency kit."

2. Pack all the items in a small container or "emergency kit." Advantages of a kit include being able to find items quicker; it is easier to check the contents; and it is easier to verify the presence of the kit in your clothing.

Recommended personal protection items include:

- High-quality pocketknife with at least two cutting blades
- Match-safe with matches
  —Waterproof plastic or metal container with waterproof kitchen matches (cushion the heads from friction)
  —Waterproof matches rolled in paraffin-soaked muslin in an easily opened container such as a small soap box, a toothbrush holder, etc.
- Needles—an assortment, at least one heavy duty. Each needle can be magnetized to serve as an emergency compass. Have heavy duty thread fastened to several needles to save threading.
- Assorted fish hooks in heavy foil
- Wire
- Needle-nosed pliers with side-cutters
- Bar of surgical soap (small)
- Small fire starter of proforic material (For suggested BSA "Hot Spark" in containers, see chapter 8.)

- Personal medicines
- Water purification materials
- Bandages and other simple first-aid supplies; butterflies, gauze, etc.
- Insect repellent stick (if necessary in your area)
- Lip balm

These are the suggested minimum essentials. Look them over and decide what items you will carry. Make sure you know how to use each one. Sewing a small kit in a parka may be a good idea. Consider the following: shelter, fire, direction, water. What items might make a good kit better? Where will you carry it?

Appendix D

Sample Agenda: A Cold-Weather Camping Weekend

Friday afternoon

3–5 p.m.   Arrive at camp.

Establish sleeping arrangements in cabins—keep heat low!

6 p.m.   Prepare evening meal. (See suggestions in the *Fieldbook*, *Cooking* merit badge pamphlet, or this handbook.)

7:30–9 p.m.   Review cold-weather training:

1. Shelter

2. Clothing

3. Sleeping arrangements

4. Winter meal planning

9:30–10 p.m.   Have a fellowship and get-acquainted time with a high-energy snack.

10:30 p.m.   *Taps.*

Saturday morning

7 a.m.   Prepare breakfast.

9 a.m.–noon   Travel to campsite location, using proper clothing and travel techniques (see chapter 7).

Noon   Lunch—be sure to include plenty of liquids.

1–3 p.m.   Activity time (hiking, skiing, snowshoeing, or snow structure building).

3–4:30 p.m.	Winter skills demonstration or competition.
5 p.m.	Prepare evening meal.
7:30–9:30 p.m.	Fellowship (excellent time for a "Nying Fire").
10 p.m.	*Taps.*

Sunday morning

7 a.m.	Prepare breakfast.
9–10 a.m.	Quiet time; worship service.
10–11 a.m.	Break camp and return to cabins. Clean up and prepare for returning home.
Noon	Hot meal with awards presentations after the meal.
	Check out with camp officials and have a safe trip home.

Appendix E

Sample Agenda:
Cold-Weather Camping
Leader Training

These materials should be sent to the participant when a reservation has been received:

1. Cold-weather camping equipment list
2. Resource inventory, to be completed and brought to class
3. Local weather information, as necessary

Time Schedule

Day 1

2–4 p.m.	Arrival and check-in.
5 p.m.	Housing assignment and issue of necessary equipment.
6 p.m.	Dinner.
or	
7 p.m.	Arrival.
7–9 p.m.	Welcome, visuals and program on course objectives. Hand out course materials.
9–10 p.m.	Get-acquainted cracker barrel.

Day 2

7 a.m.	Breakfast.
8 a.m.	Introduction. "The Fun of Cold-Weather Camping." "Your Body and the Cold." "Clothing and Sleeping Systems for Cold-Weather Camping."
Noon	Lunch.
1:30 p.m.	Group needs for cold-weather camping.
2 p.m.	"Cold-Weather Camping Shelter."
4–5:30 p.m.	"First aid in cold weather."
6 p.m.	Evening meal. Trading Post and static equipment displays.
7:30 p.m.	Evening program (recreational winter film, workshops on equipment making).
9:30–10 p.m.	Cracker barrel.

Day 3

7 a.m.	Breakfast.
8 a.m.	"Cold-Weather Food Requirements." 1. Nutrition 2. Energy value of foods 3. Water and liquid intake 4. Preparation
10 a.m.	"Cold-Weather Travel." 1. Hiking 2. Skiing or Snowshoeing 3. Using Sleds in Snow Country
11 a.m.	Evaluation and questions.
Noon	Recognition luncheon. Depart for home after checking out with program officials.

Appendix F

Trail and Camp Sanitation

(These health and safety procedures have been approved by the Health and Safety Service at the BSA national office.)

Camping leaves its mark on boys. Campers leave their imprint on places and people. Fortunately, most Scouts and Explorers are efficient campers. And efficient campers have one sure trait—they *know* and *practice* healthful field sanitation. They *know,* because their adult leaders have taught them; and they *practice,* because these leaders set the example and follow through until the practicing is a habit and a matter of pride.

Experienced leaders place a high priority on proper training in hike and camp sanitation. In using these skills, patrols and Explorer groups learn that teamwork is the key to lighten otherwise arduous jobs. Many hands make light work of camp "housekeeping," especially of those tasks essential for cleanliness and good health.

Take camp cleanup or dishwashing as one example. It can be fun— if it doesn't take too long. Otherwise it will be unpopular and a sorry job, never done well. So make it a challenge (as explained later) instead of a chore.

The principal elements of camp sanitation are personal cleanliness; safe drinking water; food care and preparation; dishwashing; disposal of waste water, garbage, and trash; and latrines.

Personal Cleanliness

Even on a hike or camping trip boys can be clean when it counts. Soap and water scrubbing is particularly important before cooking, handling of eating utensils, eating, and after using toilet facilities.

A lightweight plastic or canvas wash basin should be standard personal equipment for every camper. The only time one may not be needed is when a permanent campsite has washing facilities. Even there, cooks should improvise means for an occasional hand wash or rinse right in the "kitchen," as the need arises during preparation of a meal.

When a group camps along a running stream or lake, soap washing should never be done there. This causes water pollution. A quick dip to rinse off the trail dust after a hard day's hike or a short, supervised swim—fine. But this is not the place for soap bathing. Bathe regularly—every day, if possible. Showers are usually provided at established council, public, and private camps. In a temporary camp, set up and use an improvised method for bathing.

A blanket airing pole or line is a real asset to your camp. Dry, aired-out blankets or sleeping bags give a warm night's sleep. Clammy, musty blankets are a small comfort. Turn your bedding inside out and air it daily, weather permitting.

Safe Drinking Water

An adequate and convenient supply of safe drinking water is necessary for a successful camp or hike. You must either know the water to be safe or take necessary steps to make it safe to drink. If you are not sure, check with someone who knows the area—a park ranger or conservation officer, for example.

All water should be considered unsafe for drinking, unless it comes from a recognized or tested water system. Clear, sparkling appearance is no guarantee of water that is safe for drinking; you can't be sure unless the water has been tested recently. Well water from farms or isolated dwellings may be perfectly acceptable to the residents who have built up an immunity to its impurities, but it may be unsafe for you.

If there is any question, boil water used for drinking or treat it with water-purification tablets to be sure. If you use the boiling method, bring the water to a rolling boil and keep it there for 5 minutes. Then aerate it by pouring from one container to another to improve the taste. Always go prepared to purify water, even if it appears you may not need to do so.

Besides being sure of a safe water supply, you must also see that it is stored only in safe containers. At an undeveloped site you may have to pack in your own water. Bring it in the type of containers shown on the right.

Plastic water jugs

Food Handlers and Storage

The personal cleanliness of food handlers is a must. Cooking buddies should always wash their hands before starting meal preparation and during cooking if their hands become soiled. Always wash hands after using the latrine.

Prevent food contamination. Protect foods from dirt, water, tainting from soap, oils, and odoriferous foods such as onions, garlic, oranges, melons, and cucumbers. Seal all such foods in plastic or foil. Never save leftovers for a later meal because they may become poisonous. Eat it up or throw it out!

Avoid using foods needing refrigeration, except when camping at a permanent site that has refrigeration. Substitute nonperishable foods. If you do use perishable foods, buy them as late as possible before departure and use them up quickly. Poultry and fresh meat may have to be repacked, even for refrigerator storage. Foods that are frozen solid when taken out of refrigeration will retain their freshness and safety for a longer time.

Animal and insect foragers can be problems. Avoid feeding them— intentionally or accidentally. Chances are, they will be sniffing around soon enough. Don't encourage them. A clean camp is your best protection against unwanted animal and insect guests.

Unless you want your camp-out cut short, better make sure that your edibles are hung up out of the reach of animals. In a more permanent camp, a solid food box is a good idea. Styrofoam ice chests are not strong enough for protection. They can be easily torn apart by a hungry animal.

Food bag

Keep all food—including cookie and candy snacks—out of your tent and pack. Canvas tents and sleeping bags are no barrier to bears, who love sweets, as do raccoons, porcupines, armadillos, skunks, and many other animals and insects. They also love campers who store food in cardboard cartons in tents, on tables, or on the ground.

Patrol Dishwashing

Good dishwashing techniques involve everyone, both cleanup Scouts and other patrol members. All have responsibilities. A patrol dishwashing operation will not take longer than 20 to 25 minutes when it is a *teamwork* job. Except for the two cleanup Scouts, everyone can finish in 5 or 6 minutes. The cleanup crew sets up and supervises the operation, but each patrol member takes care of washing and rinsing his own personal eating gear. Here are the steps:

The first thing cooks should do as they start the meal is to put a large pot of water over the fire. This is to be used for hot drinks, soups, cooking, etc., during the meal preparation. This pot is refilled with water and placed over a good hot fire *before* the patrol sits down to eat.

Dishwashing is a four-part activity: scraping, washing, rinsing, and sanitizing. Scrape dishes thoroughly. Food particles, particularly grease, should be removed from dishes and cutlery until they are "sight-clean" before they are placed in the wash water.

Wash with a good detergent in clean water at a temperature of about 45° C (112° F). The wash water should not be so hot that it will be uncomfortable to the hands, but it needs to be hot enough to remove grease and food.

Rinse in clean warm water. This rinse is for the purpose of removing detergents or soap. It, too, should be warm so that the temperature of the dishes and cutlery is not lowered.

Immerse the basket of dishes for several seconds in boiling water or for 30 seconds in hot water held at a minimum temperature of 82° C (180° F) to assure disinfection.

Allow the dishes and cutlery to air-dry. If the utensils are rinsed at the prescribed water temperature, they will dry in about 1 minute. *Don't use a towel on them*. A towel that is not clean will contaminate the utensils and undo the good work that has already been done.

With a minimum of water and a soft metal scouring pad or abrasive cloth, the cleanup crew washes out the inside of all pots. They wash and rinse the cook pots, then place them near the fire to dry. An important tip on pot washing: **Soap the outside of pots before using them over an open fire; it makes scouring easier.**

Store the dishes and cook pots in a dry, flyproof place such as a patrol food box, plastic bags, or equipment pack.

Clean up fireplaces and police the area. Clean, hang up, or put away all dishwashing equipment in a place where it will dry out thoroughly. Check the fire before leaving to be sure that it is *completely* out. Douse with water and stir it with a stick. Remember: This whole process is easily completed by a well-organized patrol in less than a half hour!

FOR CLEANUP SCOUTS	FOR OTHER SCOUTS

1. Boil full pot of water. Use some for washing and the rest for rinsing.	1. Each Scout wipes off his own eating utensils.

2. Mix part of the boiling water with liquid soap and cold water for washing.	2. He washes them in a pot of wash water.

3. Add sterilizing agent to the remaining hot water for rinse water.	3. He rinses them in a pot of rinse water and then sterilizes them in a pot of boiling water.

4. While other Scouts wash their utensils, cleanup Scouts clean cooking pots.	4. He air-dries utensils on a plastic sheet and stores them in a flyproof container.

Garbage and Trash Disposal

If you camp in a public park, garbage disposal is no problem. Put garbage and other refuse in the cans provided—and do it after every meal. If cans are not provided, burn it after mealtime. First, burn everything that will burn. Next, dry out any "wet" garbage on hot stones or sticks laid across the fireplace over the remainder of your cooking fire. Once it is dry, add fuel to the fire to complete burning.

Wash or burn out all food cans, after removing both ends. Flatten them to conserve space in your tote-litter bag. Wash out jars. Don't bury any trash, cans, paper, or garbage. It probably will be dug up by animals after you leave the campsite.

Every patrol should have tote-litter bags with disposable plastic liners to carry out all unburnable trash and garbage. These are easily made by lining a cloth or heavy paper bag with a plastic bag which is closed with a rubber band or twist sealer.

The bags are carried out in the campers' packs where food was carried in. Dispose of the inner bag with trash and garbage at the nearest disposal can or take it all the way home. Do not bury it.

The Philmont Scout Ranch ranger says, "When on the trail, don't throw or bury. What you can't burn, be sure to carry—and all the way home, if necessary."

Tote-litter Bag

Waste Water Disposal

Carefully screen out all food particles and add to drying garbage before disposing of the dishwater. If you're on a permanent camp that has established water disposal sumps, use them. Temporary, small hole sumps are no longer recommended at overnight, trail, or outpost campsites for erosion prevention reasons. Wash water may be poured out next to a stump or scattered evenly across the campgrounds *after all food particles have been removed*. Do not pour it into the latrine.

Latrines

At developed campsites latrines are provided. Use them and do your share to keep them neat and clean. When camping out on a wilderness trail, farmer's land, or any primitive place where toilet facilities are not available, dig a straddle pit latrine as shown on page 147.

Dig a trench with vertical walls, only slightly wider than the span of a standard trench shovel (6-8 inches), approximately 18 inches deep, and about 36 inches long or longer depending on the duration of your stay.

A latrine should be the *only hole you make* at a campsite. Dig it away from trees to avoid roots. Pile the topsoil along one side of the trench, leaving room for foot space. Shovel part of the subsoil on a plastic sheet and carry it to the fireplace to make a hearth of unburnable dirt. Leave enough soil at the latrine so that, after each use, a light covering of dirt can be scattered in with a scoop or trench shovel.

Locate the latrine at least 100 feet from the tents and kitchen area, and away from any stream, spring, or lake to avoid drainage pollution. Choose a location that has some privacy. Take advantage of natural screening such as bushes, or screen it with a tarpaulin. Place toilet paper nearby, off the ground on a forked stick and covered by a tin can or plastic bag to keep it dry. Nearby, rig a water bag or gallon can to provide quick soap wash and hand rinse after using the latrine. Also, hang a kerosene lantern to mark its location in the dark.

When you're breaking camp and closing the latrine, bring back the borrowed subsoil from the fireplace hearth and also ashes and charred wood to fill the trench. Make certain that all fire debris has been drowned, stirred, and positively put *out*.

Replace the original topsoil and leave the trench slightly mounded. Otherwise, later settling of the soil will leave one of those marks of a poor camper—the vestige of a trench that will cause erosion.

You can always tell what kind of a camper has been there by the marks he leaves—or lack of them. Show your Scouts or Explorers how to live in camp, so they'll go home healthier than they arrived. Make them so proud of the campsite they leave that they'll want to come back to it.

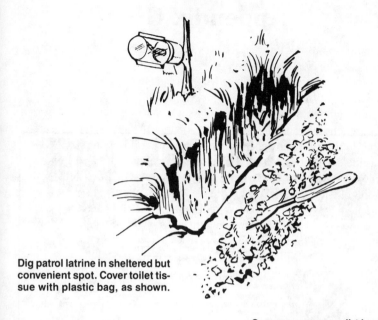

Dig patrol latrine in sheltered but convenient spot. Cover toilet tissue with plastic bag, as shown.

Carry away excess dirt in plastic sheet to kitchen area to build up nonburnable soil base for fireplace. Return dirt to latrine when striking camp.

Appendix G

Boys' Life Reprints

BEAR PAW SNOWSHOES

MONTAGNAIS — INDIAN TYPE

BY BEN HUNT

Bear-paw snowshoes are fine for rough and wooded country. They are light in weight and are easily carried on a pack when they are not being worn.

STRAPPED TO A PACK

Cut a straight hickory, ash or elm sapling 3½ inches at the butt end and at least 7 feet long.

Rip it through the center and trim it down to size, using a drawknife for roughing and a spokeshave for trimming.

Bend them around the form before they dry out. Green wood bends nicely.

ROUND PIECES OF LOG, NAILED TO PLANK

5½ D

SPREADER 9½

10 × 6

BLOCK TO PREVENT SPLINTERING

BLOCKS HOLDING ENDS

FORM can be made like this

21½

N.B. You will save yourself a lot of time and trouble if you first make a full size drawing of a snowshoe on paper

or it can be sawed out of a 2" plank like this

5½ R
9½
13¾
6¾
2¼ R

ORDER OF OPERATIONS

1. Make a form – either style.
2. Rip sapling for frames.
3. Shape with drawknife and spokeshave.
4. Bend around form while green.
5. While frames are drying on form, make crossarms.
6. Remove frames when dry and tie end temporarily.
7. Cut mortises and set cross arms.
8. Wrap spliced end with wet rawhide and let dry.
9. Drill ⅛" holes for lanyard.
10. You are now ready for webbing.

WEBBING WITH WET CALF RAWHIDE

11. Thread ⅛" lanyard through holes in toe.
12. Weave diagonals, A to AA, B to BB & C to CC and knot.
13. Weave in cross strands & fasten with half hitches.
14. Put in cross thongs X-X.
15. Weave body section, starting at 1 and follow through carefully as shown.
16. Now you can wrap X-X.
17. Thread cross thongs in heel using an awl to spread up and down thongs.

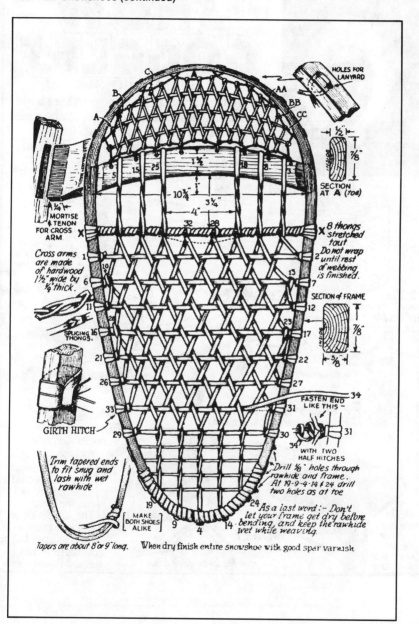

HOLES FOR LANYARD

AA
BB
CC

A B C

SECTION AT A (70%)

½"
⅞"

25 1.5 25 1½" 18 8 3

10¾" 1"
3¼"
4"

32 28

X 8 thongs stretched taut
Do not wrap until rest of webbing is finished.

X MORTISE & TENON FOR CROSS ARM.
¼"

Cross arms are made of hardwood 1½" wide by ½" thick.

SECTION of FRAME
⅞"
⅜"

SPLICING THONGS.

GIRTH HITCH

FASTEN END LIKE THIS —

WITH TWO HALF HITCHES

Drill ⅛" holes through rawhide and frame.
At 19·9·4·14 & 24 drill two holes as at toe

Trim tapered ends to fit snug and lash with wet rawhide

MAKE BOTH SHOES ALIKE

As a last word :— Don't let your frame get dry before bending, and keep the rawhide wet while weaving.

Tapers are about 8' or 9" long.   When dry finish entire snowshoe with good spar varnish.

SNOW GOGGLES

BY W. BEN. HUNT, HALES CORNERS, WIS.

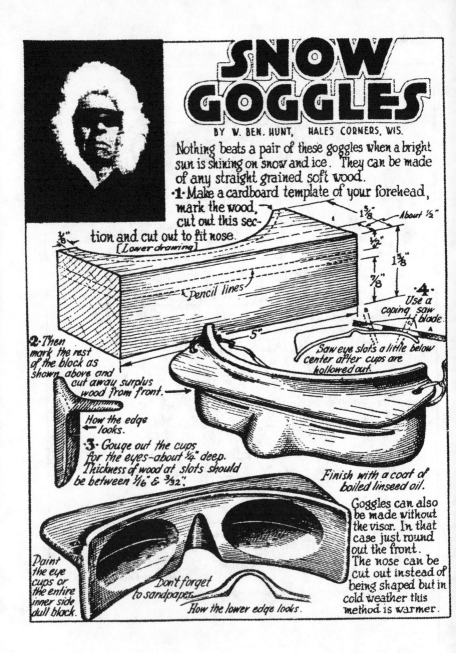

Nothing beats a pair of these goggles when a bright sun is shining on snow and ice. They can be made of any straight grained soft wood.

1. Make a cardboard template of your forehead, mark the wood, cut out this section and cut out to fit nose. [Lower drawing]

⅛"

Pencil lines

1⅜"

About ½"

½"

1⅜"

⅞"

5"

4. Use a coping saw blade.

Saw eye slots a little below center after cups are hollowed out.

2. Then mark the rest of the block as shown above and cut away surplus wood from front. →

How the edge looks.

3. Gouge out the cups for the eyes—about ¼" deep. Thickness of wood at slots should be between 1/16" & 3/32".

Finish with a coat of boiled linseed oil.

Paint the eye cups or the entire inner side dull black.

Don't forget to sandpaper.

How the lower edge looks.

Goggles can also be made without the visor. In that case just round out the front. The nose can be cut out instead of being shaped but in cold weather this method is warmer.

Bibliography

A general bibliography follows the chapter bibliographies.

Chapter 1: The Fun of Cold-Weather Camping

Cameron, Agnus and Parnall, Peter. *Nightwatchers.* New York: Four Winds Press.

Cary, Bob. *Winter Camping.* Irving, Texas: Boy Scouts of America, 1979.

"Cold-Weather Camping" in *Camping Sparklers,* Vol. 1, No. 1, No. 3686. Irving, Texas: Boy Scouts of America, 1986.

Danielsen, John. *Winter Hiking and Camping.* Glens Falls, N.Y.: Adirondack Mountain Club, 1986.

Kochanski, Mors L. *Northern Bush Craft.* Lone Pine Publishing.

Manker, Ernst. *People of the Eight Seasons.* AB Nordbok, 1975.

Polar Manual. U.S. Navy.

Rustrum, Calvin. *Paradise Below Zero.* New York: Macmillan, 1968.

Vallentine, Victor F. and Vallee, Frank G. *Eskimo of the Canadian Arctic.* McClelland and Stewart Ltd., The Carlton Library, 1968.

Winter Camping. New York: Boy Scouts of America, 1927.

Winter Scouting Handbook. Ottawa: Boy Scouts of Canada.

Chapter 2: Your Body and the Cold

Cold Facts for Keeping Warm. U.S. Army.

Cold: Physiology, Protection, and Survival. Springfield, Va.: National Technical Information Service manual AD-787 011, 1974.

Curtis, Sam. *Harsh Weather Camping.* Durham, N.C.: Menasha Ridge Press, 1986.

Fear, Eugene H. *Surviving the Unexpected Wilderness Emergency.* Olympia, Wash.: Emergency Response Institute, 1979.

Information That Can Save Your Life. Woolrich, Pa.: Woolrich, Inc.

Johnson, James Ralph. *Advanced Camping Techniques.* New York: David McKay Co., 1967.

The Most Important Energy You Save . . . May Be Your Own. Woolrich, Inc.

Outdoor Living: Problems, Solutions and Guidelines. Tacoma Mountain Rescue.

Physiology of Cold Weather Survival. Springfield, Va.: National Technical Information Service AGARD report R-620, 1974.

Wind Chill Chart. U.S. Superintendent of Documents.

Chapter 3: Clothing and Sleeping Systems

Cunningham, Gerry. *Making Your Own Equipment.* Gerry, Inc.

Fieldbook. Irving, Texas: Boy Scouts of America, 1984.

Lamoreaux, Marcia and Lamoreaux, Bob. *Outdoor Gear You Can Make Yourself.* Harrisburg, Pa.: Stackpole, 1976.

Wilder, Edna. *Secrets of Eskimo Skin Sewing.* Edmonds, Wash.: Alaska Northwest Publishing, 1976.

Chapter 4: Food, Water, and Sanitation

Angier, Bradford. *Wilderness Cookery.* Harrisburg, Pa.: Stackpole, 1961.

Barker, Harriett. *Supermarket Backpacker.* Chicago: Contemporary Books, 1977.

Best and Taylor's Physiological Basis of Medical Practice. 11th edition. Baltimore: Williams and Wilkins, 1984.

Composition of Food. Washington, D.C.: U.S. Government Printing Office.

Davis, Adelle. *Let's Eat Right to Keep Fit.* New York: New American Library, 1988.

Hunter, Beatrice. *Consumer Beware!* New York: Simon and Schuster, 1972.

Jack, Nancy. *The Complete Provisioning Book.* St. Petersburg, Fla.: Trend Books, 1978.

Jacobsen, Michael and Lerza, Catherine. *Food for People, Not for Profit: A Source Book on the Food Crisis.* New York: Ballantine, 1975.

Lappe, Francis Moore. *Diet for a Small Planet.* New York: Ballantine, 1975.

Reuben, David. *Save Your Life Diet.* Tenth anniversary edition. New York: Ballantine, 1982.

Williams, Roger. *Nutrition Against Disease.* New York: Bantam, 1973.

Winter, Ruth. *A Consumer's Dictionary of Food Additives.* New, revised edition. New York: Crown, 1984.

Chapter 5: First Aid

Auerbach, Paul S. and Geehr, Edward G. *Management of Wilderness and Environmental Emergencies.* New York: Macmillan, 1983.

Breyfogle, Newell D. *The Common Sense Medical Guide and Outdoor Reference.* Second edition. New York: McGraw-Hill, 1988.

First Aid. Merit badge pamphlet. Irving, Texas: Boy Scouts of America, 1988.

Forgey, William W. *Hypothermia—Death by Exposure.* Merrillville, Ind.: ICS Books, 1985.

Forgey, William W. *Wilderness Medicine.* Third edition. Merrillville, Ind.: ICS Books, 1987.

Kodet, E. Russel and Bradford, Angier. *Being Your Own Wilderness Doctor.* Harrisburg, Pa.: Stackpole, 1975.

Pozos, Robert S. and Wittmers, Loretz E., Jr., eds. *The Nature and Treatment of Hypothermia.* Minneapolis, Minn.: University of Minnesota Press, 1983.

Wilerson, James A. *Medicine for Mountaineering.* Seattle, Wash.: Mountaineers Books, 1967.

Chapter 6: Shelters

Anderson, Lou. "Building Eskimo Snow Houses," *Off Belay.* February, 1973.

Brower, David. *The Sierra Club Manual of Ski Mountaineering.* New York: Ballantine Books.

Provencher, Paul. *The Complete Woodsman.* Habitex Books, 1974.

"Snow Camping," *Nordic World Magazine,* World Publications, 1974.

Wik, Ole. *Wood Stoves.* Edmonds, Wash.: Alaska Northwest Publishing, 1977.

Chapter 7: Travel

Barnett, Steve. *Cross-Country Downhill and Other Nordic Mountain Skiing Techniques.* Boston: Globe Pequot Press, 1983.

Bauer, Erwin A. *Cross-Country Skiing and Snowshoeing.* Winchester, 1975.

Bennett, Margaret. *Cross-Country Skiing for the Fun of It.* Reprint of 1973 Dodd, Mead edition. Van Nuys, Calif.: Sugarfree Center.

Brady, Michael and Skjemstad, Lorns. *Ski Cross Country.* Dial Press, 1974.

Brady, Michael and Skjemstad, Lorns. *Waxing for Cross-Country Skiing.* Wilderness Press, 1979.

Caldwell, John. *Cross-Country Skiing Today.* Lexington, Mass.: Stephen Greene Press, 1977.

Caldwell, John. *The New Cross-Country Ski Book.* Lexington, Mass.: Stephen Greene Press, 1976.

Colwell, Robert. *Guide to Snow Trails.* Harrisburg, Pa.: Stackpole.

Dog Transportation. U.S. Army field manual 25-6.

Hollatz, Tom. *The White Earth Snowshoe Book.* St. Cloud, Minn.: North Star Press, 1975.

Jaeger, Ellsworth. *Tracks and Trailcraft.* New York: Macmillan Company, 1948.

Jensen, Clayne. *Winter Touring.* Edina, Minn.: Burgess, 1977.

Lederer, William J. *The New, Complete Book of Cross-Country Skiing.* New York: W. W. Norton, 1983.

Lederer, William J. and Wilson, Joe Pete. *Complete Cross-Country Skiing and Ski Touring.* W. W. Norton, 1975.

Osgood, William E. and Hurley, Leslie J. *The Snowshoe Book.* Lexington, Mass.: Steven Greene Press, 1983.

Prater, Gene. *Snowshoeing.* Third edition. Seattle, Wash.: The Mountaineers Books, 1988.

Reischl and Freman. *Ski Touring for the Fun of It.* Lexington, Mass.: Little, Brown and Company, 1973.

Tejada-Flores, Lito. *Backcountry Skiing.* San Francisco: Sierra Club, 1981.

Chapter 8: Making Equipment

How to Build Cross-Country Skis. Saskatoon Area Council, Boy Scouts of Canada, 1974.

General Bibliography

Bridge, Raymond. *The Complete Snow Camper's Guide.* New York: Charles Scribner's, 1973.

Brower, Charles. *Fifty Years Before Zero.* New York: Dodd, Mead, 1942.

Brown, Terry and Hunter. *The Concise Book of Winter Camping.* Vanguard, 1978.

Canadian Scout Handbook. National Council, Ottawa: Boy Scouts of Canada.

Cary, Bob. *Winter Camping.* Irving, Texas: Boy Scouts of America, 1979.

Down But Not Out. Information Canada.

Dunn, John M. *Winterwise: A Backpacker's Guide.* Lake George, N.Y.: Adirondack Mountain Club, 1988.

Fieldbook, Irving, Texas: Boy Scouts of America, 1984.

Freuchen, Peter. *Book of the Eskimos.* New York: Fawcett, 1981.

Goode, Merlin. *Winter Outdoor-Living.* New Brighton, Minn.: Brighton Publications, 1978.

Jaeger, Ellsworth. *Wildwood Wisdom.* New York: Macmillan, 1966.

Keithahn, Edward L. *Alaskan Igloo Tales.* Edmonds, Wash.: Alaska Northwest Publishing, 1974.

Lansing, Alfred. *Endurance: Shackleton's Incredible Voyage.* New York: Carroll and Graf, 1986.

Mohney, Russ. *Wintering: The Outdoor Book for Cold Weather Ventures.* Harrisburg, Pa.: Stackpole, 1976.

Nordic World Editors. *Winter Safety Handbook.* Mountain View, Calif.: World, 1975.

The Official Scoutmaster Handbook. Irving, Texas: Boy Scouts of America, 1981.

Osgood, William E. *Wintering in Snow Country.* Lexington, Mass.: Stephen Greene Press, 1978.

Prater, Gene. *Snowshoeing.* Seattle, WA: The Mountaineers, 1974.

Riley, Michael J. *Don't Get Snowed.* Great Lakes Living Press, 1977.

Roberts, Harry. *Movin' On.* Boston, MA: Stone Wall Press, 1977.

Rolands, John J. *Cache Lake Country.* New York: W. W. Norton, 1978.

Rossit, Edward A. *Snow Camping and Mountaineering.* New York: Funk and Wagnalls, 1974.

Rustrum, Calvin. *Paradise Below Zero.* New York: Collier Books, 1968.

Stebbins, Ray. *Cold Weather Camping.* Chicago: Contemporary Books, 1979.

Stefansson, Vilhjalmur. *The Arctic Manual.* Westport, Conn.: Greenwood Press, 1974.

Stefansson, Vilhjalmur. *My Friendly Arctic: The Story of Five Years in Polar Regions.* Westport, Conn.: Greenwood Press, 1943.

Stefansson, Vilhjalmur. *My Life With the Eskimos.*

Stefansson, Vilhjalmur. *Unsolved Mysteries of the Arctic.* New York: Mac-Millan, 1962.

Stokes, Donald W. *A Guide to Nature in Winter.* Boston: Little, Brown and Company, 1976.

This is the Arctic. Scandinavian Airlines System.

Watts, May T. and Tom. *Winter Tree Finder.* Berkeley: Nature Study Guild, 1970.

Wolfram, Gerry. *Walking Into Winter.* New York: John Wiley and Sons.

Addresses

Boy Scouts of America
Supply Division
1325 West Walnut Hill Lane
P.O. Box 152079
Irving, TX 75015-2079

National Cold-Weather Camping Development Center
Northern Tier High Adventure Programs
P.O. Box 509
Ely, MN 55731

National Council, Boy Scouts of Canada
Supply Service
P.O. Box 515
Station F
Ottawa, Canada D2C 3G7

Notes

Notes